2024 Astrology Pocket Planner from Planetary Calendar
By Ralph & Lahni DeAmicis

Planetary Calendar, an Imprint of
Cuore Libre Publishing
Napa, California
www.PlanetaryCalendar.com

ISBN 979-8-389997-98-1 on Amazon 978-1-931163-76-7 Ingram

Cover Photo Credits: NASA & ESA, John T. Clarke
(Boston University), Zolt G. Levay (STScl)

The Planetary Calendar is calculated in Solar Fire using Pacific 'Clock Time', so it adapts to Daylight Savings Time. Adjustments for the other North American time zones are found at the bottom of the 'Month at a Glance' pages. The charts are calculated for Sacramento, the capitol of California. We use this region not only because it is the center of our universe, but because the North Bay is one the longest continuously occupied regions in North America, so it clearly has good Feng Shui!

Disclaimer: Even though we make every effort to get the correct information into the correct places, there are thousands of data points, so errors occur. Also, we make every effort to provide trustworthy forecasts, based on generally accepted Astrological principles, but forecasting is, by its nature, subject to undetected influences that may skew the results. Therefore, we accept no responsibility for any losses or inconveniences you may suffer from using this information, although we truly hope you find it helpful.

Welcome to the Planetary Astrology Calendar

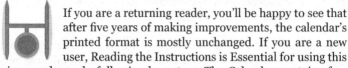

If you are a returning reader, you'll be happy to see that after five years of making improvements, the calendar's printed format is mostly unchanged. If you are a new user, Reading the Instructions is Essential for using this unique and wonderfully simple system. The Calendar contains features and annotated forecasts, supported by monthly videos, to make this information quickly accessible, whatever your level of astrological knowledge. To help you with that, there are additional graphics and videos at *PlanetaryCalendar.com/instructions*. **Note**: All versions of the Planetary Calendar include the monthly calendar pages with the English language ephemeris and symbol guide, annotated forecasts, instructions, an annual scientific ephemeris and Quick Reference Pages. The Day Planner and Digital Version, which is a navigable PDF for use on phones and computers, also include the Lunation Astrology Charts. The Day Planner features 'Week at a Glance' pages for note writing and adds the Solar Ingress charts, plus occasional bonus chapters. Many readers have more than one version of the Planetary Calendar, because knowledge is power, especially when it's handy!

Strategizing the Year Ahead: First, avoid planning events like weddings, parties or surgeries during the two-week Eclipse periods because they are often tumultuous. If you have Planets or Angles at those Degrees, take special care during those times. This is especially true this year between March 25th and April 8th when the **Great American Solar Eclipse** crosses the USA from Texas to Maine, impacting Aries and Libra. The next eclipse pair happens on September 17th and October 2nd affecting Virgo, Pisces and Libra.

These four eclipses highlight fairness, justice, partnership, human rights and spiritual belief. Mercury Retrogrades: There are three this year, each three weeks long, starting in April, August and late

November. If possible, during those nine weeks avoid purchases of phones, transportation and electronics. Refer to the Retrograde and Eclipse tables on the Quick Reference Pages.

A Look at the Year Ahead: A hard-working January deals with stalled communications as Mercury picks up speed. But with so many Planets moving Direct and Jupiter in comfort loving Taurus, cooperating with Saturn in compassionate, visionary Pisces, expect solid progress and a stable economy. Venus has no Retrogrades this year, so the Venus Ruled Signs, Taurus and Libra's interests like resources, art, partnership and justice will progress without pause. After the February 10th Aquarius New Moon (the Chinese New Year, ***Enter the Wood Dragon***) push big projects ahead until June when the economics will change due to Jupiter being newly in Gemini while Saturn in Pisces turns Retrograde. By the high Summer multiple societal planets will be Retrograde, so global politics and economics will stall. Fortunately, this will feel quite remote for most folks, so disconnect from the frustrating news and focus on your close circle and local community to find the best allies.

Uranus in Taurus continues to highlight climate issues, while Saturn in Pisces points out our vulnerable coast lines, where most people live and thrive. This reflects the philosophical divergence we are seeing between how the youngest and oldest generations want society to operate, between commercial greed and responsible stewardship of the natural world. This conflict is amplified by the **Second Great American Eclipse** that we've seen in two years, and Pluto crossing back and forth between Capricorn and Aquarius for the first time since 1778, the early days of the American Republic. *Wishing You Good Stars in this Interesting Year Ahead.*

Ralph & Lahni DeAmicis

Two: Using the Calendar

Start by looking at the whole Day Block and divide it into four quadrants. When there are more Planetary Glyphs above the Date Number (Lunar Aspects) it indicates an easier social day. More Glyphs below make for a challenging day. More Glyphs above the Dotted Line (Planetary Aspects) indicate helpful connections in the outer world. Aspects below indicate challenges.

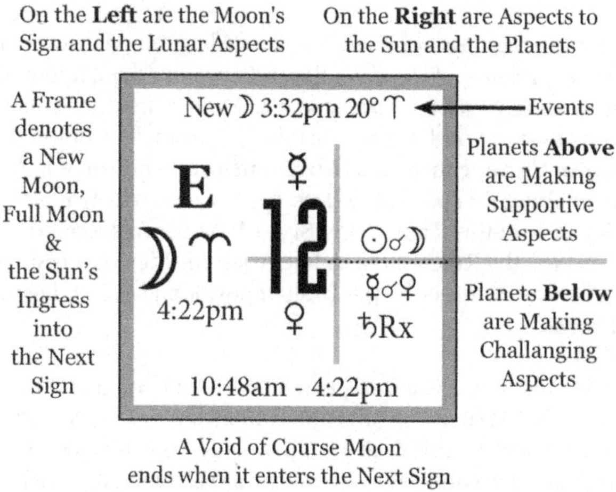

These four quadrants reflect the design of the human body. The upper body optimistically focuses on the future while the lower deals with the results. Your head thinks, 'Let's go for a walk', but it's your feet that are sore later! The left side of the body is the Lunar, emotional side, while the right is the Solar, more social side. The left is where you hold a baby's head, so they hear your heartbeat, but it's your right hand that you extend in greeting.

The 'upper' supportive Aspects are the Conjunction (0 degrees), Sextile (60 degrees) and Trine (120 degrees). The 'lower' or challenging Aspects are the Square (90 degrees) and the Opposition (180 degrees). When a day has mostly supportive Aspects, we mark it with a White Circle. When the challenging Aspects dominate, we put a Black Box around the Date. A Gray Frame found on a Day Block denotes the New Moon, Full Moon and the Sun's entrance (Ingress) into the next Sign. You can read about the Aspects to better understand their diverse influences on page 17.

Find your Sun Sign, Ruling Planet, and its Glyph on page 84 to personalize your experience of the Calendar. When your Glyph appears above the Date, the day will feel easier as the Moon supports your talents. When it is below, you have to work harder to make things come out right. **Note: Cancer and Leo Sun Positions.** The Sun and Moon do not appear above and below the Date, so Cancerians instead use Venus, the Ruler of feminine Taurus, the Sign of the Moon's Exaltation. The Leos use Mars, the Ruler of masculine Aries, the Sign of the Sun's Exaltation. The way we describe the Exalted position is as the 'Best Friend' or "Colleague".

When your Planetary Ruler appears above or below the Dotted Line, that Planet is making a significant connection with another Planet, indicating important things are happening in your life. While Aspects above the Line are supportive and below are challenging, the nature of the Planets and the Aspect that connects them will shape how it affects you. Planetary Aspects are felt for extended periods and the slower the Planet, the longer the duration of those effects. For example, Mercury to Venus Aspects may last a few days, while Saturn to Neptune Aspects can last weeks or longer. Read the pages about the Planets and the Aspects for a greater understanding of those differences.

Three: Reading the Calendar Layout

The Upper Page

On either side of the Month and Year you will see the Signs that begin and end each month. Below that is the Forecast with the Capital Footnote (A) referencing the Dates on the Grid. The Forecast provides insights into the Planetary Transits, Direction changes (Retrograde or Direct) and Aspects. At the bottom of the page is the Glyph to English Key with Keywords to make understanding the calendar easier. See the expanded descriptions of the Signs, Planets and Aspects on pages 13 to 18.

The Lower Page

The Compact Text Ephemeris shows the Planetary Positions by Sign and Degree on the first day of the month, in plain language. It also shows any Planetary Sign changes and direction changes (Retrograde or Direct). There is a classic Table Ephemeris for the year after December, but the Compact Ephemeris is a quick reference for Planetary positions. At the bottom margin are calculations for four continental USA Time Zones. The Calendar is calculated for Pacific 'Clock' Time. There is no need to adjust your calculation for Daylight Savings Time unless your State does not use it.

The only Lunar Aspects shown on the line are to the Sun. The Planetary Direction changes are also shown on the Dotted Line, 'D' for Direct is above the line and 'Rx' for Retrograde is below. The White Circle denotes a day with mostly supportive Aspects, when new projects encounter minimum resistance. The Black Box around the Date denotes a day with challenging Aspects when new projects may require extra work. A Gray Frame denotes the Lunations.

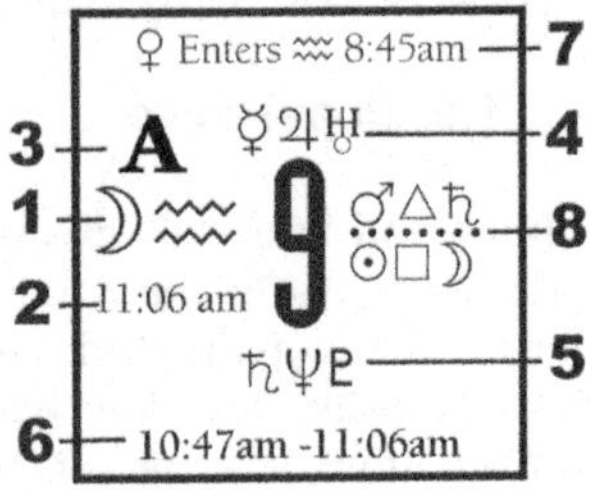

What the Day Blocks Signify

Use the Date in the center as your reference

1) To the left is the symbol for the Moon and its current Sign.
2) Below that is the time when the Moon enters that Sign.
3) Above that is a letter that footnotes to the forecast. e.g '**A**'.
4) Above are the supportive Aspects (Conjunction, Sextile, Trine).
5) Below are the challenging Aspects (Square, Opposition).
The Lunar Aspects Above & Below the Date run
from left to right, as they occur from early to late.
6) At the lower edge of the Box are the times of the Moon's Void of Course (VOC) see pg. 31, which can span multiple days.
7) At the top edge of each box are the Planetary Ingresses, Lunations, Eclipses, Meteors and Holidays.
8) To the right of the Date on the Dotted Line are the Planetary Aspects. Supportive Aspects are above and Challenging Aspects are below. Their time sequence runs from the Dotted Line up or Dotted Line down, with the earliest Aspects touching the Line.

Four: Text Ephemeris, Planetary Speed & VOC

The Text Ephemeris is easy to read because everything is in English and each planets motions are described. There is a full Ephemeris after December for long range planning. The Text Ephemeris shows the month's Planetary Movements, Sign and Direction changes, with degrees. The Solar and Lunar changes are shown in the Day Blocks. The Sun entering a new Sign and the New Moon and Full Moon are highlighted with a Gray Frame.

Mercury☿ 10° Capricorn♑ enters Aquarius♒ on the 13th at 9:51am. Venus♀Rx 20° Capricorn♑. Mars♂ 21° Scorpio♏ enters Sagittarius♐ on the 13th at 1:52am. Jupiter♃ 25° Aquarius♒ enters Pisces♓ on the 28th at 8:09pm. Saturn♄ 8° Aquarius♒. Uranus♅Rx 11° Taurus♉. Neptune♆Rx 20° Pisces♓. Pluto♇ 25° Capricorn♑.

Start projects between the New and Full Moon because energy is rising. The Sun Trine Moon after the Full Moon (Waning Gibbous) is when the energy is flowing most smoothly so that's a good time to overcome resistance. As Planets prepare to change Direction they slow from our perspective and issues related to them in our world will be harder to move forward.

When the Planets are moving fast, you have the wind at your back. Everything related to them happens more quickly and easily. That is why it is important to understand what each Planet signifies. In our Forecasts, we also take into account the speed of the Planets as indicators.

Some Planets change Sign and Direction more often. Here is a quick guide to each Planet's orbit.

Mercury: 88 days; **Venus**: 224.7 days; **Earth**: 365.256 days; **Mars**: 687 days; **Jupiter**: 11.86 years; **Saturn**: 29.5 years; **Uranus**: 84 years; **Neptune**: 164.8 years; **Pluto**: 248 years

While the inner Planets affect our daily lives, outer Planets affect our social standing. For example, Jupiter Returns to your birth position at ages 12, 24, 36, etc., often lucky years. Saturn takes 29.5 years to 'Return', once the average lifespan, thus Saturn's connection to maturity. The current lifespan is 78 years, closer to the orbit of Uranus, although with its 84-year orbit, many people never experience their Uranus Return. Our experience of Uranus, Neptune and Pluto, with their long orbits, is less personal and more gradual, often intangible. We imagine them like our utilities; they exist in the background and we don't notice them until the power, water or internet go out.

About the Void of Course (VOC) Moon

The period after the Moon's last Aspect to any Planet, until it enters the next Sign, is the Void of Course. Imagine the Moon as someone running between meetings who finds themselves at loose ends until the next. While this time may be potentially unproductive, it can also be a very creative time because it lacks an agenda. Also, some VOC periods are better than others. When the Moon is in Signs Ruled by Jupiter (Sagittarius & Pisces) or its own Rulership & Exaltation, (Cancer & Taurus) she is self-directed and resourceful so that time is less challenging.

Five: About the Signs

To use the Calendar effectively you will need to know your Sun Sign and its Ruling Planet. It's important to understand what the Twelve Signs represent beyond the annual sequence of nature's seasons.

Planets are defined in four ways and each is a unique combination of those definitions: Polarity, Element, Quality and Planetary Ruler. The two Polarities are Masculine and Feminine. We can also call them Dynamic and Responsive.

Then there are the Four Elements: Fire, Earth, Air and Water. These represent the four States of Matter in physics: Plasma, Solid, Gaseous and Liquid. Masculine Fire energizes, Feminine Earth stabilizes, Masculine Air interacts and Feminine Water dissolves.

The Three Qualities represent the stages within the annual cycle of the seasons: Cardinal initiates, Fixed systemizes and Mutable humanizes.

The Planets are related to the Signs in complex ways described by the Table of Planetary Dignities. Each Planet has six Signs that it relates to most directly, but in the Calendar we want you to use what is called the Planet's 'Ruling' Signs, the most socially active Dynamic and Responsive positions.

We use the classic, traditional Rulers, so there are no Rulerships assigned to Uranus, Neptune or Pluto. If you learned Astrology in the fifties, sixties and seventies, this may seem bizarre but the Astrologers who assigned the 'modern' Rulers had limited understanding of the underlying Geometry at work. They also had almost no data on the newly discovered Planets to base those decisions.

That means both **Aries** and **Scorpio** will look for **Mars** above or below the Date and Dotted Line in the Day Blocks as an indicator about the day. **Sagittarius** and **Pisces** will look for **Jupiter**. **Capricorn** and **Aquarius** will look for **Saturn**.

The Twelve Signs

Planetary Ruler, Quality, Element, Action, Opposite Sign

♈ **Aries**: ♂ Mars, Cardinal, Fire, Initiates, ♎
The symbol is the Ram. They are energetic.
♉ **Taurus**: ♀ Venus, Fixed, Earth, Stabilizes, ♏
The symbol is the Bull. They are patient.
♊ **Gemini**: ☿ Mercury, Mutable, Air, Interacts, ♐
The symbol is the Twins are in arm. They are engaging.
♋ **Cancer**: ♂ Moon, Cardinal, Water, Nurtures, ♑
The symbol is the Crabs. They are protective.
♌ **Leo**: ☉ Sun, Fixed, Fire, Creates, ♒
The symbol is the Lion. They are dramatic.
♍ **Virgo**: ☿ Mercury, Mutable, Earth, Perfect, ♓
The symbol is the Virgin. They are diligent.
♎ **Libra:** ♀ Venus, Cardinal, Air, Balances, ♈
The symbol is the Scales. They are considerate.
♏ **Scorpio**: ♂ Mars, Fixed, Water, Manages, ♉
The symbol is the Scorpion. They are daring.
♐ **Sagittarius**: ♃ Jupiter, Mutable, Fire, Optimizes, ♊
The symbol is the Centaur's bow & arrow. They are confident.
♑ **Capricorn**: ♄ Saturn, Cardinal, Earth, Codifies, ♋
The symbol is the Sea Goat. They are dependable.
♒ **Aquarius**: ♄ Saturn, Fixed, Air, Innovates, ♌
The symbol is the Water Bearer. They are revolutionary.
♓ **Pisces**: ♃ Jupiter, Mutable, Water, Unites, ♍
The symbol is the Fishes. They are philosophical.

Six: About the Planets

The Calendar shows the every changing dynamics between the Planets and how they influence us through these Aspects. Our descriptions of the Planets are about the nature of the energy that they bring to those meetings. To understand the Planets you need to see them in their various guises and that is what our Table of Dignities reveals. In the same way that we act differently at work or home, with friends or family, the Planets each have six roles they play on the Astrological stage. They have three Social roles: the two Rulers and the Exaltation, and three Personal roles: the two Detriments and the Fall.

To learn more, read the Calendar's Companion Book for a non-misogynistic explanation of this vital interpretation tool. To that end, we have replaced Masculine and Feminine with Dynamic and Resposive. When Planets are in Aspect, the 'current' is flowing. If you jump into projects when the Aspects are Supportive, you can ride the tides. If you start when they are Challenging, you'll be bucking the flow.

How Planets Act When they Make a Connection

When the **Sun** makes an Aspect, it brings energy to that Planet. When Supportive, it promotes stability. When Challenged, it bullies. The Sun's Dynamic Ruling Sign is Leo; Cancer is its Receptive Ruler and Aries is its Exaltation. In those Signs, the Sun lives for the outer, social world. In the opposite Signs, Aquarius, Capricorn and Libra, the Sun is concerned for the personal life.

When the **Moon** makes an Aspect, it lends emotional oomph to the relationship. Supportive; it's a helping hand. Challenged; it's a slap. The Social Trilogy is Cancer, Sagittarius and Taurus. The Personal Trilogy is Capricorn, Gemini and Scorpio.

When M**ercury** connects it promotes engagement. Supportive; it provides good information. Challenged; it teases and tests.
When **Venus** connects, beauty and indulgence arrive. Supportive; it's graceful and artistic. Challenged; it is indulgent.
When **Mars** connects passions heat up. Supportive; it is protective, engaging. Challenged; defensive, destructive.
When **Jupiter** connects horizons, possibilities & imagination expand. Supportive; it rescues. Challenged; it runs roughshod.
When **Saturn** connects it provides maturity, discipline, structure. Supportive; a protective wall. Challenged; a limiting fence.
When **Uranus** connects it electrifies, networks & communicates. Supportive; it is a community. Challenged; it is a gang.
When **Neptune** connects it expands us beyond the visible. Supportive; new levels of perception. Challenged; confusion.
When **Pluto** connects it amplifies, intensifies. Supportive; strong gets stronger. Challenged; magnifies the weaknesses.

Seven: About the Aspects

Aspects are the angles made between the Sun, Moon, Planets, Ascendant and Midheaven. As an Astrological tool, it's like a family tree crossed with a wiring diagram. While individual Planets show a person's talents, the Aspects show the Planets either working in concert (Conjunct 0°), being mutually supportive (Sextile 60° & Trine 120°), or being demanding (Square 90° & Opposition 180°). A less used Aspect is the Parallel, that shows when Planets have a similar status.

Conjunction - 0 to 7 Degrees - The Planets are close together, deciding and working in concert.

Sextile - 60 Degrees - Polarity, the Sextile creates an easy, supportive relationship, like cousins working and playing together.

Square - 90 Degrees - Imagine cars meeting at an intersection. The drivers must use the rules and their wits to get where they're going and avoid crashing.

Trine - 120 Degrees - This harmonious, strongly supportive connection is like siblings who provide the muscle and resources each other needs without question.

Opposition - 180 Degrees - Imagine two people sitting opposite each other negotiating. While each is committed to their position, they need something from each other.

Parallel - 0 degrees of Latitude - This notes Planets equally North or South of the Ecliptic, holding equal status, or rank. By itself it's not significant, but it eases the way for any other Aspect. The related Aspect, the Contra Parallel, which is marked by the parallel lines with an angled line crossing them, represents Planets at opposite distances above and below the Ecliptic. This describes a mentor relationship in which the lower Planet is the beneficiary of the upper. We don't list the Contra Parallel, although we consider it in our forecasts.

When evaluating Aspects, consider what each Planet does for the other:

The Sun energizes, the Moon comforts,
Mercury engages, Venus charms,
Mars confronts, Jupiter expands,
Saturn compresses, Uranus disrupts,
Neptune envisions and Pluto empowers.

The Aspects determine how they contribute. The Conjunction unifies. The Sextile and Trine help without causing trouble. The Square and Opposition build and noisily bang into each other, because that's the nature of work.

The Aspects involving the Sun, Moon, Mercury, Venus, Mars and the Ascendant are felt personally. Those involving Jupiter, Saturn and the Midheaven are experienced socially. Aspects involving Uranus, Neptune and Pluto are felt gradually, because they change Signs so slowly, maintaining Aspects for long periods.

Outer planet Aspects are like sitting on a boat deck with friends and a big bottle of wine, enjoying the afternoon turning into evening. As the tide rolls in and the boat gradually rises, no one notices. It's only later, as they step down to the dock, that they'll recognize the change. Outer Planet Aspects are a different experience from the inner Planetary Aspects that say, *'Bam! Wake Up, Mars is Here!'*

Eight: About the Calendar's Astrology

The calendar's simplified astrology uses three components: the Planets, who are the actors, the Signs of the Tropical Zodiac, that describe the actions, and the geometric Aspects that are the relationships between the Planets. The fourth major part of an Astrological Chart is the House System, that brings the Planets down to Earth. While we use Whole Sign Houses when creating the written Forecasts, they are not considerations in the data we put in the Day Blocks.

An Astrological Chart is a cosmic weather report. In the same way that a TV meteorologist tells you the current weather based on a specific time and place we calculate Astrology Charts for the exact minute. Just like weather forecasts, Astrology forecasts are based on the laws of physics and observation.

Astrologers have been observing the influence of the heavenly Planets on the Earth below for thousands of generations. The Astronomical ephemeris shows us where the Planets will be in the future, and we can look for when those patterns appeared in the past. When we know what happened historically at that time, we get clues about possible events in the future.

Astrology Calendars are different than Charts, because they are about the ongoing movement of the Planets and the relationships they form and dissolve during the evolving year. In the forecasts, we make a big deal when a slow-moving Planet like Jupiter, Saturn or Pluto changes Sign, because a long-running agenda in larger economic or social movements is going to change.

The information in the Day Blocks include the major Planets and the traditional Aspects: Conjunctions, Sextiles, Squares, Trines, Oppositions, plus Parallels. In the written forecasts we add the major Asteroids and Chiron and rely on our own Table of Dignities, to show how the Planets perform in diverse Signs. We prefer that to the highly misogynistic table that came to us from Medieval times.

Our table is based on Sacred Geometry and it includes dual Rulers for the Sun and the Moon, a concept that was always in the Astrology of Ancient Greece. You can read more about that in the Calendar's companion book. To prepare the calendar, we generate data reports of the major Aspects, charts for all the Solar Ingresses and Lunations and Astro*Carto*Graphy maps using the current Solar Fire Software.

The Amicis Table of Dignities

Celestial Body	Dynamic Ruler	Responsive Ruler	Exalted Sign	Dynamic Detriment	Responsive Detriment	Fall Sign
☉	♌	♋ (V)	♈	♒	♑ (V)	♎
☾	♐ (V)	♋	♉	♊ (V)	♑	♏
☿	♊	♍	♒	♐	♓	♌
♀	♎	♉	♓	♈	♏	♍
♂	♈	♏	♑	♎	♉	♋
♃	♐	♓	♋	♊	♍	♑
♄	♑	♒	♎	♋	♌	♈
⚳	♊	♍	♏	♐	♓	♉

Dotted Line Designates a Primary Sign & V a Vice Sign. www.SpaceAndTime.com (C) 2018 R & L De Amicis

Nine: BioDynamic Gardening

Biodynamic organic farming was developed in the 1920's in response to the wide-scale use of chemicals in farming following WWI. It uses an Astrological Gardening Calendar to time tasks in the field.

Water Moon Days are good for leaf plants like lettuce, spinach, celery and cabbage. Cancer, Scorpio, Pisces.

Fire Moon Days are good for fruits, nuts, seeds and gourds like cherries, pumpkins, oranges. Aries, Leo, Sagittarius.

Earth Moon Days are good for root vergetables and storing crops. Taurus, Virgo, Capricorn.

Air Moon Days are good for flowering plants and medicinal herbs like mints and basil. Gemini, Libra, Aquarius.

The New Moon is for resting, celebration and meditation.

The Full Moon is for celebration and harvesting all crops, especially medicinal plants.

Wine Tasting

The flavors of wine come from the fruit and are perceived through the nose and palate. Both the Fire (Fruit) Moon (Aries, Leo, Sagittarius) and the Air (Flower) Moon (Gemini, Libra, Aquarius) tend to bring out the subtle, more nuanced notes in the wines. The Earth Moon (Taurus, Virgo, Capricorn) favor serious, aged wines with deep earthy qualities, while the Water Moon (Cancer, Scorpio, Pisces) can add a lighter, smoother quality, loosening up an otherwise stiff varietal wine. See our book, 'Wine Tasting with the Stars' for more.

THE SPACE & TIME CATALOG

Planetary Calendar Astrology

Moving Beyond Observation Into Action

This calendar companion book explains our practical, simplified approach using illustrations and analogies to show how the chart's geomety and symbolism tell a story. . Illustrated, 172 pages, $20.00

Wine Tasting with the Stars

The 2024 Astrology Tasting Calendar

Wine and Astrology are two enjoyable and illuminating topics that have been linked since when wine was the only health drink and electric lights didn't hide the night sky. Astrology is a tool for describing how nature and society is organized and it can help us easily understand the personality of the most popular wine grapes. We also explain how our experience of wines changes with the Moon Signs. This includes the Planetary calendar pages. 76 pages - 12 ounces - 8.5" X 5.5" by .5" $15.00

Feng Shui and the Tango

The Essential Chapters - 25th Anniversary Editon

Excerpts from the popular three book series 106 pages, $17.00

It takes over 6 months to create the calendar from prep, setup, calculations, data input, forecasting, proofing and upload to our printer. We weather multiple transits, including at least one Mercury Rx, to get the calendars ready for you. They say, "best laid plans..." but once it gets to the printer, we can only hope they're having good transits. We got the calendar off early in 2022 only to be hit with printer delays. We breathe a sigh of relief when we finally get our hands on them so we can deliver them to you! Since 2020, our cover photos are chosen from the NASA archives to remind us that we are the receivers for all the signals sent toward us by those big radio transmitters in the galaxy we affectionately call the planets! Sometimes supportive, often challenging, always giving us new information to assimilate.

Find More by Ralph & Lahni www.PlanetaryCalendar.com

Ordering Next Year's Planetary Calendar

Calendars are ready in the Summer of the current year. Advance orders are mailed as soon as the Calendars are available when pre-paid with a check, money order or credit card. Please include your contact info in case there are questions about your order.
For International orders please email us for a shipping quotes at Sales@SpaceAndTime.com before ordering.

Order Online at www.PlanetaryCalendar.com

In the USA: XL Wall $20.00 Original Wall $18.00
Mini Pocket $15.00 Day Planner $22.00
Digital for Cell Phones & Tablets $14.00

U.S. Funds Only - No additional shipping fees required.

MAIL ORDERS TO:
Planetary Calendar
PO Box 5391 Napa, CA 94581-0391
For Phone Orders or Customer Service Please leave a Voicemail with Email at **(800) 217-4197** - *We respond Quickly!*

We accept AmEx, Disc, MC and Visa via Phone & Online.
Credit card orders require full name, billing address, phone number & email along with credit card #, exp date, & security code.
Please allow 4-6 weeks for delivery (Although they are typically shipped immediately). We are not responsible for postal delays.

Planetary Calendar Since 1949

January Forecast

The month will move along at a good pace thanks to only Uranus being Retrograde. With Mercury coming off Station to turn Direct on the 1st, issues related to communication may be off to a slow start. Don't worry, by February, Mercury will be moving at a good clip and those issues will resolve. With Mars, Mercury and Venus sequentially moving into Capricorn your determined hard work will yield especially good results. The year is winding down towards the Lunar Spring festival at the Aquarius New Moon on February 9th, when the Earth's energy is most withdrawn. That will begin the Year of the Wood Dragon so use January to tie up any loose ends hanging over the past year. We suggest you complete any traveling before that date because the following week is ideal for staying close to home and putting everything in order.

(A) The practical Capricorn Sun Trine the Virgo Moon is perfect for moving projects ahead and Mercury turning Direct in the visionary part of Sagittarius, Conjunct Mars, makes this a good time to enthusiastically broadcast your plans for the year ahead to others. Capricorns, watch your temper until Mars enters Aquarius on February 12th. **(B)** Mars forges ahead into Capricorn with good Aspects to Jupiter and Saturn, so focus your physical energy and passion on practical achievements that satisfy your heart and soul. Capricorn celebrates while Cancer hibernates. **(C)** This is a cozy day to get together with your intimate friends and family and talk about serious subjects, including sex, if you have strong Scorpio in your chart.

(D) This is a low key, New Moon; go beyond your own interests and pay attention to world events. Sagittarians, depend on your charm rather than your wit.

(E) This highly social day could lead to financial opportunities or employment thanks to Jupiter Trine Mars. Good for the Earth Signs.
(F) Mercury enters hardheaded Capricorn so consider those serious decisions carefully.
(G) This is a soulful day for connecting with your senior guides and wise spirits beyond the physical, especially for the Water Signs.
(H) This very social day is a great time to prepare a meal or have lunch with someone you care about of a different generation, and share stories of the family's history. Grandparents and grandkids are natural allies. Great for the Earth Signs.
(I) The Sun and Pluto enter Aquarius on the same day while the Sun supports the Moon. This is a profound time, especially for the Air Signs, infuse yourself with light, both natural and spiritual.
(J) Venus enters sensual and ambitious Capricorn; take your pleasures seriously. Capricorn; expect to feel more attractive.
(K) This Full Moon challenges us to think and plan like global citizens. This is a good time for the Fire Signs.
(L) Get those forgotten and neglected tasks done, and enlist help if necessary. You've got the wind at your back and helpers are willing.
(M) And, make sure you buy your helpers lunch, because it will be a fun and productive weekend.

• •

Mercury ☿Rx 22° Sagittarius♐ turns Direct on the 1st at 7:07pm at 22°Sagittarius♐, enters Capricorn♑ on the 13th at 6:49pm.
Venus♀ 3° Sagittarius♐ enters Capricorn♑ on the 23rd at 12:50am.
Mars♂ 27° Sagittarius♐ enters Capricorn♑ on the 4th at 6:57am.
Jupiter♃ 5° Taurus♉. Saturn 3° Pisces.
Uranus♅Rx 19° Taurus♉ turns Direct on the 26th at 11:34pm at 19°.
Neptune♆ 25° Pisces♓.
Pluto♇ 29° Capricorn♑ enters Aquarius♒ on the 20th at 4:50pm.

Signs

♈ Aries Begins
♉ Taurus Owns
♊ Gemini Engages
♋ Cancer Nurtures
♌ Leo Embraces
♍ Virgo Improves
♎ Libra Commits
♏ Scorpio Manages
♐ Sagittarius Views
♑ Capricorn Climbs
♒ Aquarius Herds
♓ Pisces Dreams

Planets

☉ Sun Spirit
☽ Moon Emotes
☿ Mercury Thinks
♀ Venus Feels
♂ Mars Acts
♃ Jupiter Expands
♄ Saturn Contracts
♅ Uranus Disrupts
♆ Neptune Envisions
♇ ⯓ Pluto Unearths

Aspects

☌ Conjunct 0° Aligns
∥ Parallel 0° Equals
⚹ Sextile 60° Helps
□ Square 90° Works
△ Trine 120° Supports
☍ Opposition 180° Counters

JANUARY 2024

<table>
<tr><th>Sunday</th><th>Monday</th><th>Tuesday</th></tr>
<tr><td></td><td>New Year's Day
A ♅ ☿'D' ☉∥♇ ☉△☽
☽♍ 1
♀□♄</td><td>♇
☽♎ 2
4:46pm ☿♆♂
3:35pm - 4:46pm</td></tr>
<tr><td>Orthodox Christmas Day
♆♇♇♂ ☉∥☽
☽♐ 7
1:08pm ♄
12:21pm - 1:08pm</td><td>♀
☽♐ 8
☿□♆</td><td>☿ ☉△♅ ♂⚹♄
☽♑ 9
5:33pm ♆
10:24am - 5:33pm</td></tr>
<tr><td>♄♃♂♄
☽♓ 14</td><td>Martin Luther King
G ♅♆♆♇ ☉⚹♆ ☉⚹☽
☽♈ 15
8:48pm ♀
8:32pm - 8:48pm</td><td>☽♈ 16
☿♂</td></tr>
<tr><td>☽♊ 21 ☿∥♇</td><td>☽♋ 22
1:50pm ♆♀
12:39pm - 1:50pm</td><td>♀ Enters ♑ 12:50am
J ♄♃
☽♋ 23
☿♂</td></tr>
<tr><td>M ♃ ♀△♃ ☿△♅
☽♍ 28</td><td>♂♅☿ ♂△♅
☽♍ 29
♆
3:19pm ---------</td><td>N ♇♆ ☉△☽ ♂∥♇
☽♎ 30
12:03am ♀
--------- 12:03am</td></tr>
</table>

All calculations are Pacific Clock Time (PST & PDT)

Capricorn the Sea Goat to Aquarius the Water Pourer

Wednesday	Thursday	Friday	Saturday
3rd Quarter ☽ 7:30pm ♀♆ ☽♎ 3 ☉□☽	♂ Enters ♑ 6:57am Quadrantid Meteors B ☿ ☽♎ 4	♄♂♄ ☽♏ 5 4:39am ♇♃ 3:40am - 4:39am	Epiphany - 3 King's Day Astrologer's Day C ♀☿ ☽♏ 6 ☉⚹☽ ♅
♄♂♃ ☽♑ 10	New ☽ 3:57am 20° ♑ D ♅♆♇ ☉∥☿ ☽♒ 11 ☉☌☽ 7:01pm 6:32pm - 7:01pm	♂♇☿♀♀ E ☉∥☽ ☽♒ 12 ♂△♃ ♃	☿ Enters ♑ 6:49pm F ☿ ☽♓ 13 ☉∥♀ 7:28pm ♅ 1:58am - 7:28pm
1st Quarter ☽ 7:52pm ♀ ☽♈ 17 ☉□☽	♃♄☿♃♂♅ H ☽♉ 18 ☿⚹♄ 12:11am ♇ 12:02am - 12:11am	♅♆ ☽♉ 19 ☿△♃ ♀□♆	☉ Enters ♒ 6:07am ♇ Enters ♒ 4:50pm I ♇ ☽♊ 20 ☉△☽ ☉☌♇ 5:57am ♄ 5:56am - 5:57am
♅♆ ☽♌ 24 11:36pm ♇ 2:57pm - 11:36pm	Full ☽ 9:53am 5° ♌ K ☽♌ 25 ☉☍☽ ♃ Tu B'Shevat	☽♌ 26 ♅ 'D' ☉□♃ ♅ 1:19pm ----------	L ♃♀ ♀⚹♄ ☽♍ 27 ☿∥♇ ☿☌♂ 11:11am ♄ ---------- 11:11am
☽♎ 31 ☿∥♀ ♂	**Notes**		

Add 1 Hour for Mountain Time (MT)) Add 2 Hours for Central Time (CT) Add 3 Hours for Eastern Time (ET)

February Forecast

All the planets are traveling Direct, which helps projects and relationships move forward rapidly. This pattern repeats in April. Also, Mercury has accelerated, easing communication and on the 4th, it moves into the Exalted Sign of Aquarius, so group and electronic conversations become energized. The Aquarius New Moon on the 9th is the time when the Earth's energy field is most withdrawn, after which seeds in the northern Hemisphere become active. It affects people too and the week following the Lunar New Year is the ideal time to stay home and clean out last year's debris and create a fresh start for the year ahead.

(A) Mercury enters Aquarius meeting an even smaller Planet, Pluto. Be especially vigilant with your computer and phone security. Watch for nation-station sponsored computer viruses on the world wide web. The Air Signs may become light sensitive during Mercury's transit so if sleep is disrupted make your bedroom darker.

(B) A very social day, spend it with those who share your beliefs and entertain alternate ideas and relationships.

(C) The Wood Dragon is not a ferocious beast, but a creature of the sky, luminous and dependable. Choose relationships for their durability and practical satisfaction. Expect to hear about the climate's impact on people playing in the background all year long. The greatest fortune will go to those who align their strategies and actions according to their deeply held beliefs. Watch our video forecast for more. **(D)** Mars joins Pluto, Mercury and the Sun in Aquarius, showing that when many small, individual voices are united they possess transformative power. Speak up, because that may bring you like-minded allies.

(E) Smooth transits make this a suitable time to start new projects and relationships. Good for the Air Signs, and Aries.
(F) Watch out for chaos in your relationships, other's greediness may upset you. Be careful with whom you share your feelings.
(G) The Sun enters Pisces, leaving behind four planets in Aquarius and joining Saturn, so be prepared to fit your dreams and aspirations into practical, restrained vehicles. That 'down to earth' thinking will help turn them into reality.
(H) Mercury enters Pisces, the position of the great mathematicians. Be prepared for illumination and write down your ideas and inspirations because this is the time for 'big thoughts'. Good for the Water Signs. **(I)** At this Full Virgo Moon you can get a great deal done, especially on projects that will yield long term benefits, but be prepared to work diligently. If you are not prepared to make an effort, avoid starting anything new. Gemini, and Sagittarius will feel challenged.
(J & K) There are numerous productive Aspects on both days, BUT, there is a two day Void of Course Moon in Libra that could cause extensive distractions and indecision. Plan these days carefully and follow your list to get the most done. Especially rough for the Air Signs.
(L) An excellent day for moving projects and relationships ahead, especially for the Water Signs.

Mercury☿ 24° Capricorn♑ enters Aquarius♒ on the 4th at 9:09pm, enters Pisces♓ on the 22nd at 11:28pm.
Venus♀ 11° Capricorn♑ enters Aquarius♒ on the 16th at 8:04am.
Mars♂ 20° Capricorn♑ enters Aquarius♒ on the 12th at 10:04pm.
Jupiter♃ 7° Taurus♉. Saturn♄ 6° Pisces♓.
Uranus♅ 19° Taurus♉.
Neptune♆ 25° Pisces♓.
Pluto♇ 0° Aquarius♒.

FEBRUARY 2024

Signs

- ♈ Aries Begins
- ♉ Taurus Owns
- ♊ Gemini Engages
- ♋ Cancer Nurtures
- ♌ Leo Embraces
- ♍ Virgo Improves
- ♎ Libra Commits
- ♏ Scorpio Manages
- ♐ Sagittarius Views
- ♑ Capricorn Climbs
- ♒ Aquarius Herds
- ♓ Pisces Dreams

Planets

- ☉ Sun Spirit
- ☽ Moon Emotes
- ☿ Mercury Thinks
- ♀ Venus Feels
- ♂ Mars Acts
- ♃ Jupiter Expands
- ♄ Saturn Contracts
- ♅ Uranus Disrupts
- ♆ Neptune Envisions
- ♇ ⯓ Pluto Unearths

Aspects

- ☌ Conjunct 0° Aligns
- ∥ Parallel 0° Equals
- ⚹ Sextile 60° Helps
- □ Square 90° Works
- △ Trine 120° Supports
- ☍ Opposition 180° Counters

Sunday	Monday	Tuesday
Notes		
☿ Enters ♒ 9:09pm A ☽♐ 4 ♄	☿☌♇ ☉⚹☽ ☽♐ 5 ♆ 9:05pm	♄♃ ☽♑ 6 4:08am 4:08am
Super Bowl ♅♀♆ ☽♓ 11	♂ Enters ♒ 10:04pm Lincoln's Birthday D ♆♂♇ ☽♈ 12 5:25am 4:31am - 5:25am	Mardi Gras E ☿ ☽♈ 13 ☉⚹☽ ♂☌♇ ♀⚹♆
☉ Enters ♓ 8:12pm G ☿ ☽♋ 18 ☉△☽ 7:24pm ♆ 7:20pm - 7:24pm	President's Day ♄♃ ☽♋ 19	♅♆ ☽♋ 20 10:37pm
♅ ☽♍ 25 ♆ 11:35pm	♇♆ ☽♎ 26 6:29am 6:29am	J ♂♀ ☽♎ 27 ☉∥☽ ♂□♃ 10:21am

All calculations are Pacific Clock Time (PST & PDT)

Aquarius the Water Pourer to Pisces the Fishes

Wednesday	Thursday	Friday	Saturday
	♄ ☽♏ 1 12:36pm ☿♇ 1:02am - 12:36pm	Groundhog Day 3rd Quarter ☽ 3:17pm ♄♀ ☉∥☽ ☽♏ 2 ☿⚹♆ ☉□☽ ♃	♂☿♀♆♂♇☿♇ ☽♐ 3 10:27pm ♅ 7:24pm - 10:27pm
B ♀♅♆♂ ☽♑ 7 ♂⚹♆ ♀△♅ 11:52pm	♇☿♇ ☽♒ 8 ☉□♅ 5:59am ♃ 5:59am	New ☽ 2:58pm 20° ♒ C ♂♀☿ ☽♒ 9 ☉☌☽ ♅ 12:35pm	Lunar New Year Year of the Wood Dragon ♄♃♄ ☽♓ 10 ☉∥☽ ☿□♃ 5:42am 5:42am
Valentine's Day Ash Wednesday ♃♄♃ ☽♉ 14 7:02am ♀♇♂ 2:20am - 7:02am	♅♅ ☽♉ 15 ☿	♀ Enters ♒ 8:04am 1st Quarter ☽ 7:00am F ♆♀♇♂ ☽♊ 16 ☉□☽ 11:39am ☿□♅ 7:00am - 11:39am	☽♊ 17 ♀☌♇ ♄
☽♌ 21 ♀☌♂ 5:40am ♇♀♂ 5:40am	☿ Enters ♓ 11:28pm H ☽♌ 22 ♃♅ 8:17pm	☽♍ 23 ☉∥♄ 5:37pm ♅☿♃ 5:37pm	Full ☽ 4:30am 5° ♍ I ♃ ☽♍ 24 ☉☍☽ ♄ ♀□♃
☉☌♄ ☿∥♄ K ♄☿ ☿☌♄ ☽♏ 28 ☉☌☿ 7:08pm ♇ 7:08pm	L ♀♄☿ ☽♏ 29 ☉△☽ ☿⚹♃ ♃♂	**Notes**	

Add 1 Hour for Mountain Time (MT)) Add 2 Hours for Central Time (CT) Add 3 Hours for Eastern Time (ET)

March Forecast

(A) This is a month when events will move quickly because the Planets are all traveling Direct. Take advantage of that because it only happens during a couple of months each year. Navigating those pathways may be tricky because so few of the Planets possess external dignities, so the month lacks clear archetypes as landmarks. Your best results will come from depending more on your intuition and imagination than on your expectations and logic. Be social and open to inspiration and you can make significant inroads. By the Spring Equinox, expect greater clarity but it will take until April before the archetypes becomes focused.

(A) The Sun Sextile Jupiter coupled with the Scorpio Moon offers a window for personal enrichment, either financially, culturally or philosophically. Good for the Water Signs. **(B)** Watch for conflicts with the people closest to you, especially among the Fire Signs. Sagittarius: speak softly. **(C)** Get together with friends and co-workers to brainstorm. That Mercury Neptune pairing in Pisces opens doors to the collective genius, especially for the Water Signs.

(D) Mercury entering Aries while Uranus engages the Sun and Mars opens the door to new ideas and innovation. What new beginnings can you implement? We are talking to you Aries! **(E)** Saturn and Neptune bracket this New Moon Conjunction so there may be a sense of restriction imposed by the outer world. Don't let that affect your personal relationships, especially among Aquarians. **(F)** Venus enters its Exalted Sign of Pisces, so your imagination and compassion become important tools. Pisces, be prepared to be pampered and adored. **(G)** The Sun Neptune Conjunction, so late in Pisces, greatly enhances our sensitivity to the global consciousness. While it is an ideal time for meditation, spend some time visualizing the world beyond yourself.

(H) The Sun enters Aries, its Exalted Sign, at the Spring Equinox. Now, with Venus and the Sun in Dignified Signs, the landmarks become prominent. The Exaltations reveal the connections the Planets make, in this case Venus connected to Jupiter, and the Sun connected to Mars, like the relationship between a favorite aunt or uncle to a niece or nephew.The best way to use them is by seeking connections. Connect your sense of fairness to your generosity and connect your spiritual energy to your physical passion. **(I)** The Saturn Venus Conjunction encourages people to formalize and demand more from their relationships. A challenging time for Virgo.
(J) Mars enters Pisces, subduing that Martial energy, although it's great for dancing. Pisces: control your temper and impulsiveness.

(K) Eclipse! Even though the Sun is in Martial Aries, this event is heavily colored by Venus. As is often true when it comes to Venus, expect the unexpected. Mysteries abound and do not be surprised when you feel like the Fool from the Tarot stepping into the unknown. The time between this and th Great American Solar Eclipse on April 8th will be an emotionally complex time. Treat yourself well.
(L) An Aries Sun Trine the Sagittarius Moon offers a period of healing. Focus on yourself and your desired vision for the future.

• •

Mercury☿ 12° Pisces♓ enters Aries♈ on the 9th at 8:02pm.

Venus♀16° Aquarius♒ enters Pisces♓ on the 11th at 2:50pm.

Mars♂ 13° Aquarius♒ enters Pisces♓ on the 22nd at 4:47pm.

Jupiter♃ 11° Taurus♉.

Saturn♄ 9° Pisces♓.

Uranus♅ 19° Taurus♉. Neptune♆ 26° Pisces♓.

Pluto♇ 01° Aquarius♒.

Signs

♈ Aries Begins
♉ Taurus Owns
♊ Gemini Engages
♋ Cancer Nurtures
♌ Leo Embraces
♍ Virgo Improves
♎ Libra Commits
♏ Scorpio Manages
♐ Sagittarius Views
♑ Capricorn Climbs
♒ Aquarius Herds
♓ Pisces Dreams

Planets

☉ Sun Spirit
☽ Moon Emotes
☿ Mercury Thinks
♀ Venus Feels
♂ Mars Acts
♃ Jupiter Expands
♄ Saturn Contracts
♅ Uranus Disrupts
♆ Neptune Envisions
♇ ⯓ Pluto Unearths

Aspects

☌ Conjunct 0° Aligns
∥ Parallel 0° Equals
⚹ Sextile 60° Helps
□ Square 90° Works
△ Trine 120° Supports
☍ Opposition 180° Counters

MARCH 2024

Sunday	Monday	Tuesday
Easter Orthodox Easter ☿ ☽♑ **31** 9:05pm ♀♆ 5:15pm - 9:05pm	**Notes**	
3rd Quarter ☽ 7:23am **B** ♂♀ ☽♐ **3** ♀□♅ ♄☿ ☉□☽	☽♑ **4** ☿⚹♅ 1:14pm ♆ 7:40am - 1:14pm	♄♃♅ ☽♑ **5** ☉⚹☽
New ☽ 1:00am 20° ♓ Daylight Saving Begins **E** ♅♆♆♇☿☿ ☽♈ **10** ☿⚹♇ ☉∥☽ ☉☌☽ 5:19pm 12:45pm - 5:19pm	♀ Enters ♓ 2:50pm Ramadan Begins **F** ☽♈ **11**	♂♀ ☽♉ **12** 5:28pm ♇ 4:07am - 5:28pm
St. Patrick's Day **G** ♀ ☽♋ **17** ☉☌♆ 2:40am -------- 2:40am	♄♃♅ ☽♋ **18** ☿	☉ Enters ♈ 8:06pm Spring Equinox **H** ♆ ☽♌ **19** ☉△☽ 12:32pm ♇ 11:52am - 12:32pm
Palm Sunday Purim ♇ ☉∥☽ ☽♎ **24** ♀⚹♃ 1:37pm ♆ 8:48am - 1:37pm	Full ☽ 12:00am 5° ♎ Appulse ☾ Eclipse **K** ♆♀ ☽♎ **25** ☉☍☽ Holi	♄♂ ☽♎ **26** ☿ 4:08pm ---------

All calculations are Pacific Clock Time (PST & PDT)

Pisces the Fishes to Aries the Ram

Wednesday	Thursday	Friday	Saturday
Notes		A ♇♆ ☽♏ **1** ☉⚹♃ ♀♅ 11:47pm --------	♇ ☽♐ **2** ☉∥☿ 5:55am -------- 5:55am
☿♆♇ ☽♒ **6** 4:38pm 11:35am - 4:38pm	♇♂ ☽♒ **7** ☿∥♆ ♃	C ♀♂♀ ☽♓ **8** ☿☌♆ 5:03pm ♅ 10:55am - 5:03pm	☿ Enters ♈ 8:02pm D ♄♃♄ ☽♓ **9** ☉⚹♅ ♂□♅
♃♄♅♃ ☽♉ **13**	♅♆♇ ☉⚹☽ ☽♊ **14** ☉∥♆ 8:15pm ♂ 3:28pm - 8:15pm	☿ ☽♊ **15** ♀♄	1st Quarter ☽ 9:10pm ♂ ☽♊ **16** ☉□☽ ♆ 9:42pm --------
☽♌ **20** ♀∥♄ ♃	Nowruz I ☿♃ ♀☌♄ ☽♌ **21** ☉⚹♇ ♅♂ 11:33pm --------	♂ Enters ♓ 4:47pm J ☿ ☽♍ **22** 12:41am -------- 12:41am	♃♅ ☽♍ **23** ♄♀
♂ ☽♏ **27** 2:02am ♇ -------- 2:02am	♄♀ ☽♏ **28** ♀⚹♅ ♃♅	Good Friday Orthodox Good Friday ♇♆♇ ☽♐ **29** 12:51pm ♂ 8:39am - 12:51pm	L ☽♐ **30** ☉△☽ ♄

Add 1 Hour for Mountain Time (MT)) Add 2 Hours for Central Time (CT) Add 3 Hours for Eastern Time (ET)

April Forecast

While The beginning of April is dominated by the **Great American Solar Eclipse** crossing the continent in an arc from Texas to Maine at midday on the 8th. This eclipse is concentrated in Pisces, Aries and Taurus, so if those are your Sun, Moon or Ascendant positions, be prepared for a demanding time. This will make the first eight days of the month emotionally intense so try to chill! After the 8th the pressure quickly comes off and the planets get feisty as the emotional debris from the Eclipse gets shaken off. As the month ends a sense of balance between the polarities returns.

(A) Mercury turns Retrograde in Aries on April Fool's Day so expect communication snafu's to pop up until the 25th when it turns Direct. Mercury Retrograde in Aries is not an especially difficult transit, although frustrating to any impatient Aries.

(B) Venus Conjunct Neptune late in Pisces is a great time to envision the beauty and balance that you wish to embody, especially for the Water Signs. **(C)** Venus enters Aries, a very internalized position when we should focus on nurturing our inner passions. Great for Aries and the other Fire Signs. **(D)** With so many planets connecting with the Moon, plan on a very socially pleasing day. **(E)** This powerful Eclipse, Conjunct Chiron, the Wounded Healer, puts the individual in touch with how their early wounds shape the person they are today. If this Eclipse contacts your chart, that area will be sensitized so you can use the time to heal often forgotten scars. Watch our monthly forecast video for April 2024 at PlanetaryCalendar.com for a deeper understanding of this event.

(F) With the Taurus Moon making multiple supportive contacts, have a meal with those you care about and be prepared to be sympathetic, because that Mars Conjunct Saturn may make any aches and pains more evident. Pisces and Virgo, be careful about overdoing physical tasks. **(G)** As the Sun enters Earthy Taurus, a group of supportive Aspects will help shake off the previous Eclipse. This is a great day for conversations on a walk to someplace different and interesting. **(H)** Jupiter Conjunct Uranus can be lucky for Taurus, especially if you depend on your intuition. Exciting things can come from distant places. **(I)** This Full Moon is dominated by Feminine Planets so you will get your best results by responding, rather than leading. Good for the Earth and Water Signs. **(J)** Finally Mercury turns Direct, after further complicating an already complicated month, so expect communications to smooth out, albeit gradually, finally getting into high gear by mid-May. Good for Aries. **(K)** Mars connecting with Neptune in late Pisces following the Sun Trine Moon, most active on the 27th, encourages you to put energy into the future you desire. Especially you Pisceans plus the other Water Signs. **(L & M)** In quick succession, Venus enters her Responsive Ruling Sign Taurus and the next day, Mars enters his Dynamic Ruling Sign Aries, so the polarities are well defined, which is a good way to end the month. Good for the Earth and Fire Signs.

••

Mercury☿ 27° Aries♈ turns Rx on the 1st at 3:14pm,
turns Direct on the 25th at 15° Aries♈ at 5:53am.
Venus♀ 25° Pisces♓ enters Aries♈ on the 4th at 8:59pm,
enters Taurus♉ on the 29th at 4:31am.
Mars♂ 7° Pisces♓ enters Aries♈ on the 30th at 8:32am.
Jupiter♃ 17° Taurus♉. Saturn♄ 13° Pisces♓. Uranus♅ 20° Taurus♉.
Neptune♆ 27° Pisces♓. Pluto♇ 01° Aquarius♒.

Signs

♈ Aries Begins
♉ Taurus Owns
♊ Gemini Engages
♋ Cancer Nurtures
♌ Leo Embraces
♍ Virgo Improves
♎ Libra Commits
♏ Scorpio Manages
♐ Sagittarius Views
♑ Capricorn Climbs
♒ Aquarius Herds
♓ Pisces Dreams

Planets

☉ Sun Spirit
☽ Moon Emotes
☿ Mercury Thinks
♀ Venus Feels
♂ Mars Acts
♃ Jupiter Expands
♄ Saturn Contracts
♅ Uranus Disrupts
♆ Neptune Envisions
♇ ⯓ Pluto Unearths

Aspects

☌ Conjunct 0° Aligns
∥ Parallel 0° Equals
⚹ Sextile 60° Helps
□ Square 90° Works
△ Trine 120° Supports
☍ Opposition 180° Counters

APRIL 2024

Sunday	Monday	Tuesday
	3rd Quarter ☽ 8:14pm Easter Monday A ♂♄ ☽♑ 1 ☿Rx ☉□☽ *April Fool's Day*	♃♅♀♆ ☽♑ 2 ☿ 10:40pm
♆♇♀♀ ☽♈ 7 4:24am 1:26am - 4:24am	New ☽ 11:20am 19° ♈ Total ☉ Eclipse E ☿ ♂∥♄ ☽♈ 8 ☉☌☽ ☉∥☽ 7:38pm	☿♃ ☽♉ 9 4:23am ♇ 4:23am
♄♂ ☽♋ 14 ☉∥☿ ♀	1st Quarter ☽ 12:12pm Tax Day ♃♅♆ ☽♌ 15 ☉□☽ 7:23pm ☿♇ 4:22pm - 7:23pm	☽♌ 16
♇♆♂ ☽♎ 21 ☉□♇	Earth Day Lyrid Meteors Peak ♄ ☽♎ 22 ☿♀ 4:23pm	Full ☽ 4:48pm 4° ♏ Passover First Day I ☽♏ 23 ☉☍☽ 8:19am ♇ 8:19am
K ♂☌♆ ☉△☽ ☽♑ 28 2:37am ♆ 12:30am - 2:37am	♀ Enters ♉ 4:31am L ♄♅♃ ☽♑ 29 ♂∥♆ ☿	♂ Enters ♈ 8:32am Passover Ends M ♆♂♇♇ ☽♒ 30 ♀□♇ 8:19am ♀ 8:18am - 8:19am

All calculations are Pacific Clock Time (PST & PDT)

Aries the Ram to Taurus the Bull

Wednesday	Thursday	Friday	Saturday
B ♇♇ ☽♒ **3** ♀∥♆ ♀☌♆ 2:07am ----- 2:07am	♀ Enters ♈ 8:59pm C ☿ ☽♒ **4** ☉⚹☽ ♃♅ 10:39pm -----	♂ ☽♓ **5** 4:12am ----- 4:12am	D ♄♂♄♃♅ ☽♓ **6** ♀⚹♇
Ramadan Ends F ♅♂♄♃♅ ☽♉ **10** ♂☌♄	♆♇♀ ☽♊ **11** ☉☌☿ 5:58am 3:03am - 5:58am	☿ ☽♊ **12** ☉⚹☽ ♄♂	☽♋ **13** 10:44am ♆ 7:45am - 10:44am
♀☿ ☽♌ **17** ♃♅	☽♍ **18** ☉△☽ 7:10am 5:01am - 7:10am	☉ Enters ♉ 6:59am G ☿ ♂⚹♅ ♂⚹♃ ☽♍ **19** ☿☌♀ ☉∥☽ ♄	H ♀♃♅ ☽♎ **20** ☿∥♀ ♃☌♅ 8:08pm ♂♆ 5:19pm - 8:08pm
♄ ☽♏ **24**	J ♇♂♆♇ ☽♐ **25** ☿'D' 6:36pm ♅♃ 4:16pm - 6:36pm	National Arbor Day ☽♐ **26**	☿♀ ☽♐ **27** ♄♂

Notes

Add 1 Hour for Mountain Time (MT)) Add 2 Hours for Central Time (CT) Add 3 Hours for Eastern Time (ET)

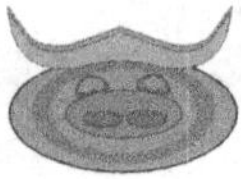

May Forecast

After a tumultuous April, due to the Eclipse, the month of May is bucolic. Although that's not to say it is uneventful. While May starts with all the planets Direct, an indicator of rapid progress, Pluto, on the far reaches of the Solar System, where the Sun would appear as a large star, turns Retrograde in Aquarius. In September it will dip back into Capricorn, finally returning to Aquarius in late November. But that's not the month's biggest event. That happens on the 25th when giant **Jupiter enters Gemini**, beginning a Square by Sign to Saturn and starting a challenging economic cycle, when the generations may have a hard time seeing eye to eye about how they work and play. Although progress through the month is steady, it's not rushed so enjoy the easy pace.

(A) Pluto Turns Retrograde early in Aquarius, so the Air Signs should be prepared for subtle shifts in their energy. **(B)** Supportive Aspects make this a good day for small accomplishments, especially for the Water Signs. **(C)** With multiple Lunar contacts expect a busy social day. **(D)** This is a pleasant and social Taurus New Moon during which unusual relationships could blossom. The continuing contact between Jupiter and Uranus keeps love and social contacts sparkling.

(E) Mother's Day is blessed with social Aspects and a cozy Sun Moon relationship that celebrates motherhood. Make sure there is as least one unusual gift in the stack. **(F)** Exciting things can be started today, but beware of 'out of the blue' surprises, that could be good or could be upsetting. **(G)** Mercury enters placid Taurus, so even though the planet is accelerating, Venus Ruled Taurus endows it with a patient grace. A good time for doing earthy, creative projects with your hands like gardening, pottery or painting, especially for the Earth Signs.

(H) The Sun is Conjunct Jupiter while Venus is Conjunct Uranus. The four planets are within five degrees of each other in late Taurus. This is a profound transit in a deeply mystical part of the sky inhabited by the Pleiades, the Seven Sisters. Healers and highly spiritual people will feel this at a deeply soulful level. Don't fall into the sorrow that comes from a sense of loss and instead, glory in the deep wisdom that comes from living a full life. **(I)** With the Sun moving into Gemini, the feeling lightens up and the Air Signs rejoice, after months that may have felt burdensome to their light filled souls. **(J)** The Full Moon in early Sagittarius, when Venus crosses Jupiter's path on the way to Gemini, rapidly expands our communication horizons. Great for Sag and Gemini. **(K)** Jupiter joins Venus and the Sun in early Gemini, Trine by Sign to Pluto in Aquarius. The struggle between the way that the different generations want to do business will continue through the rest of the year. **(L)** Memorial Day is wonderfully social and an ideal time for the generations to get together. **(M)** Take advantage of the supportive Sun Trine the waning Moon to move projects ahead. Great for the Air Signs. **(N)** With so many contacts lined up to supportively engage the Moon, watch out for getting overloaded with visits, phone calls and texts.

Mercury☿ 17° Aries♈ enters Taurus♉ on the 15th at 10:04am
Venus♀ 2° Taurus♉ enters Gemini♊ on the 23rd at 1:30pm.
Mars♂ 0° Aries♈.
Jupiter♃ 24° Taurus♉ enters Gemini♊ on the 25th at 4:14pm.
Saturn♄ 16° Pisces♓.
Uranus♅ 22° Taurus♉.
Neptune♆ 28° Pisces♓.
Pluto♇ 02° Aquarius♒ turns Rx on the 2nd at 10:46am.

Signs

♈ Aries Begins
♉ Taurus Owns
♊ Gemini Engages
♋ Cancer Nurtures
♌ Leo Embraces
♍ Virgo Improves
♎ Libra Commits
♏ Scorpio Manages
♐ Sagittarius Views
♑ Capricorn Climbs
♒ Aquarius Herds
♓ Pisces Dreams

Planets

☉ Sun Spirit
☽ Moon Emotes
☿ Mercury Thinks
♀ Venus Feels
♂ Mars Acts
♃ Jupiter Expands
♄ Saturn Contracts
♅ Uranus Disrupts
♆ Neptune Envisions
♇ ⯓ Pluto Unearths

Aspects

☌ Conjunct 0° Aligns
∥ Parallel 0° Equals
⚹ Sextile 60° Helps
□ Square 90° Works
△ Trine 120° Supports
☍ Opposition 180° Counters

MAY 2024

Sunday	Monday	Tuesday
Notes		
Cinco de Mayo ☿☿ ☽♈ **5** 10:56pm ----------	Eta Aquarid Meteors ♀ ☽♉ **6** ☉⚹♄ 2:41pm ♇ ---------- 2:41pm	New ☽ 8:21pm 18° ♉ **D** ♀♅♃♄ ☽♉ **7** ☉☌☽ ☉∥☽
Mother's Day **E** ♀♄♅♃ ☽♋ **12** ☉⚹☽ ☿	**F** ♆♂ ☽♌ **13** ♀⚹♄ ☉☌♅ 3:35am ♇ 2:12am - 3:35am	Yom Ha'atzmaut ♃♅ ☽♌ **14** ☉∥☽ ☉∥♃ ♀
♄ ☉⚹♆ ♀∥♅ ☽♎ **19** ♂ 8:48am ----------	☉ Enters ♊ 5:59am **I** ☽♏ **20** 3:33pm ♇ ---------- 3:33pm	☽♏ **21** ☿
Lag Ba Omer ☿♄ ☽♑ **26** ♂	Memorial Day **L** ♅♆♃♇♀ ☽♒ **27** ☿⚹♄ 1:44pm 1:01pm - 1:44pm	**M** ♇ ☽♒ **28** ☉△☽

All calculations are Pacific Clock Time (PST & PDT)

Taurus the Bull to Gemini the Twins

Wednesday	Thursday	Friday	Saturday
3rd Quarter ☽ 4:27am May Day / Lei Day ☿ ☽♒ 1 ♃∥♅ ⊙□☽ ♅	A ♀ ☽♓ 2 ♇Rx 11:51am ♃ 2:28am - 11:51am	B ♄♄ ⊙✶☽ ♂✶♇ ☽♓ 3	Kentucky Derby C ♅♃♆♆♇♂♂ ☽♈ 4 1:40pm 12:06pm - 1:40pm
♅♃♆♇ ☽♊ 8 4:20pm 2:55pm - 4:20pm	♂ ☽♊ 9 ♄	☿ ☽♋ 10 8:12pm ♆ 6:48pm - 8:12pm	♂ ☽♋ 11 ⊙∥♅
1st Quarter ☽ 4:47am ☿ Enters ♉ 10:04am G ♀☿ ☽♍ 15 ⊙□☽ 2:32pm ♅♃ 9:40am - 2:32pm	☿ ☽♍ 16	♀♅♂♃ ☽♍ 17 ⊙△☽ ☿□♇ ♄	Armed Forces Day H ♇ ⊙☌♃ ♀☌♅ ☽♎ 18 3:22am 2:08am - 3:22am
♄♇ ⊙△♇ ♀∥♃ ☽♏ 22 ♅	Full ☽ 6:52am 2° ♐ ♀ Enters ♊ 1:30pm J ♆♇ ♃✶♆ ♀✶♆ ♀☌♃ ☽♐ 23 1:23am ♀♃ ⊙☍☽ 12:27am - 1:23am	♂ ☽♐ 24 ♄	♃ Enters ♊ 4:14pm K ♆ ☽♑ 25 ♀△♇ 8:35am ♆ 7:46am - 8:35am
♂ ☽♓ 29 5:32pm ☿♅♃ 7:19am - 5:32pm	3rd Quarter ☽ 10:12am ☽♓ 30 ♀☌♅ ⊙□☽ ♀	N ♄♄♅☿♆♆♃♇ ☽♈ 31 8:28pm 7:54pm - 8:28pm	

Add 1 Hour for Mountain Time (MT)) Add 2 Hours for Central Time (CT) Add 3 Hours for Eastern Time (ET)

June Forecast

With so many planets moving Direct and a fast Mercury traversing its Ruling Sign Gemini, expect a fast-paced June. Although Saturn is slowing, so societal issues may coast while personal matters fly by.

(A) Mercury enters Gemini, enhancing conversations, flirting and humor. Coupled with a Taurus Moon, lunch or dinner out would be fun.

(B) This part of the week can be especially social and entertaining but avoid excess distractions. Great for the Air Signs.

(C) At the New Moon, with five Planets in Gemini and Mars in Aries, quick encounters during practical tasks and errands will be enjoyable. This is not the best time for doing the 'big stuff.'

(D) Mars enters Taurus, cooling its jets after its energetic dash through its impatient, Ruling Sign of Aries. Slow your pace to enjoy the process more. **(E)** With the Sun, Mercury and Venus traveling in late Gemini, events and conversations move quickly but watch out they don't turn into disputes, thanks to Mercury's impish side.

(F) Venus enters homey Cancer while the Libra Moon is Trine the Gemini Sun, so a great day for Fathers, although the Venus Square Neptune might produce some odd color combinations among the gifts-.A good time is beginning for Cancer, filled with love and indulgences.

(G) Mercury joins Venus in Cancer and suddenly, practical issues like food and comfort have replaced wit and flirting. Good things coming for the Water Signs.

(H) At the Summer Solstice, a page turns as those numerous Planets previously in playful, dynamic Gemini enter cozy, comfortable and responsive Cancer. With Mars and Uranus in Taurus, and Saturn and Neptune in Pisces, the feminine Planets dominate, while the Masculine Planets are scattered around the sky and disconnected.

With Saturn about to turn Retrograde while Jupiter continues to advance, the conditions are building towards a Square in August, signaling economic conflicts between companies wanting to expand into new areas and restrictive government regulations and religious objections. **(I)** The Capricorn Full Moon supports that conservative and anxious Saturn in Pisces so expect spending to become more risk averse closer to the Summer. **(J)** That White Circle marks a day with positive Lunar Aspects that are supported by the waning Moon Trine the Sun, while Mercury, in cagey Cancer, is Trine timid Saturn. To be successful at this time, projects will need to offer a clear benefit with a minimum of risk.

(K) The Black Box is for Saturn turning Retrograde. Saturn represents the structures in our life. In a house, it's the walls. In a medieval village, it's the encircling wall protecting the community. Saturn establishes limits and in Pisces, those are called the morals or beliefs that restrict us to performing primarily life-affirming actions. When it turns Retrograde, Saturn wants us to reevaluate our previous decisions, to see if they were in alignment with our beliefs. Use the opportunity to repair any gaps. For the USA, Saturn in Pisces represents the protective coastlines that guard our country, so this is a time to reconsider how we treat our beautiful and productive oceans.

• •

Mercury☿ 26° Taurus♉ enters Gemini♊ on the 3rd at 12:36am, enters Cancer♋ on the 17th at 2:06am.

Venus♀ 10° Gemini♊ enters Cancer♋ on the 16th at 11:20pm.

Mars♂ 24° Aries♈ enters Taurus♉ on the 8th at 9:34pm.

Jupiter♃ 0° Gemini♊.

Saturn♄ 18° Pisces♓ turns Rx on the 29th at 19° Pisces♓ at 12:05pm.

Uranus♅ 24° Taurus♉. Neptune♆ 29° Pisces♓.

Pluto♇ Rx 01° Aquarius♒.

Signs

♈ Aries Begins
♉ Taurus Owns
♊ Gemini Engages
♋ Cancer Nurtures
♌ Leo Embraces
♍ Virgo Improves
♎ Libra Commits
♏ Scorpio Manages
♐ Sagittarius Views
♑ Capricorn Climbs
♒ Aquarius Herds
♓ Pisces Dreams

Planets

☉ Sun Spirit
☽ Moon Emotes
☿ Mercury Thinks
♀ Venus Feels
♂ Mars Acts
♃ Jupiter Expands
♄ Saturn Contracts
♅ Uranus Disrupts
♆ Neptune Envisions
♇ ⯓ Pluto Unearths

Aspects

☌ Conjunct 0° Aligns
∥ Parallel 0° Equals
⚹ Sextile 60° Helps
□ Square 90° Works
△ Trine 120° Supports
☍ Opposition 180° Counters

JUNE 2024

Sunday	Monday	Tuesday
♂ ☽♉ **30** ☉⚹☽ ♇ 5:00am ---------- 5:00am	Notes	
♂♂ ☽♉ **2** ☿⚹♆ ♃△♇ ☿∥♅ 10:55pm 3:03pm - 10:55pm	☿ Enters ♊ 12:36am **A** ♅ ☽♉ **3** ☿△♇ ♇	**B** ☿♃♄♅♀ ☽♉ **4** ☉∥☽ ☉☌♀ ☿∥♃ ☿☌♃
♅♆♃♀ ☽♌ **9** ☉□♄ ♂♇ 12:28pm 12:05pm - 12:28pm	☿♃☿ ☽♌ **10** ☉∥☿ ☉∥☽	Kamehameha Day ♀ ☽♍ **11** ☉⚹☽ ♂□♇ ♅ 10:38pm 12:16pm - 10:38pm
♀ Enters ♋ 11:20pm Father's Day **F** ☿♀ ☽♏ **16** ☉△☽ ♀□♆ 11:37pm 11:04pm - 11:37pm	☿ Enters ♋ 2:06am Eid al Adha **G** ☽♏ **17** ☿☌♀ ☿□♆ ♇♂	♄ ☽♏ **18**
♄♅♆♇ ☽♒ **23** 8:14pm 8:05pm - 8:14pm	♃♇ ☽♒ **24** ♂	☽♓ **25** ♅ 11:07pm 3:29pm - 11:07pm

All calculations are Pacific Clock Time (PST & PDT)

Gemini the Twins to Cancer the Crab

Wednesday	Thursday	Friday	Saturday
Notes			♀ ☽♈ **1** ⊙⚹☽
♆♇♃☿ ☽♊ **5** ⊙∥♀ 1:35am 1:08am - 1:35am	New ☽ 5:37am 16° ♊ **C** ♀ ☽♊ **6** ⊙☌☽ ♄	♂ ☽♋ **7** 5:40am ♆ 5:15am - 5:40am	♂ Enters ♉ 9:34pm **D** ♄ ☽♋ **8** ♀□♄
Shavuot ♂♂ ☽♍ **12** ☿∥♀ ☿□♄ ♃	1st Quarter ☽ 10:18pm ☽♍ **13** ⊙□☽ ♄☿	Flag Day **E** ♅♇♃ ☽♎ **14** ⊙☌☿ 11:11am ♀♆ 10:53am - 11:11am	♄ ☽♎ **15**
Juneteenth ♇♆♇ ☽♐ **19** 9:31am ♅♃ 9:18am - 9:31am	⊙ Enters ♋ 1:50pm Summer Solstice **H** ☽♐ **20** ⊙□♆ ♄	Full ☽ 6:07pm 01° ♑ **I** ☽♑ **21** ☿⚹♂ ⊙☍☽ 4:08pm ♆ 3:57pm - 4:08pm	♂ ☽♑ **22** ♀☿
J ♀♂ ☿△♄ ☽♓ **26** ⊙△☽ ♃	♄♄☿♅ ☽♓ **27** ☿∥♀	3rd Quarter ☽ 2:53pm ♆♆♇♃ ☽♈ **28** ♀⚹♂ ⊙∥☿ ⊙□☽ 1:51am 1:44am - 1:51am	**K** ☽♈ **29** ☿⚹♅ ♄Rx ♀☿ 9:56pm

Add 1 Hour for Mountain Time (MT)) Add 2 Hours for Central Time (CT) Add 3 Hours for Eastern Time (ET)

July Forecast

As we move through Summer, the main event is Neptune joining Saturn and Pluto in their Retrograde motions. As more Outer Planets turn Retrograde, external societal affairs will slow or stall. However, the personal planets continue moving Direct with Mercury moving at an especially good clip so, personal lives will progress well. The month has four Circle days, when primarily supportive aspects dominate, and no Black Boxes, when the challenging aspects hold sway. That makes a low stress month in which life can move along smoothly.

(A) Mercury enters in dramatic Leo, joining the mission-focused Asteroid Vesta, so be prepared to speak from the heart. All the transits are supportive as Neptune turns Retrograde, creating a wonderful day for get togethers, meetings and initiating relationships or projects. Wonderful for the Fire Signs.

(B) The New Moon occurs close to the USA's patron star, Sirius, while Venus in Cancer is supported by Mars and Saturn.

This gives the sense of a fresh start, one that brings together home, passion and belief. Do whatever makes you feel good today, especially you Water Signs. **(C)** This is a high communication day, including multiple ways to connect to your community and world.

(D) Accomplish things that help people on a profound level, even if it's just focusing on your own health. Good for Cancer and Virgo.

(E) Venus joins Mercury in Leo, while supported by Neptune. A wonderful day to start an artistic activity. Good for the Fire Signs.

(F) Having passionate, physical Mars Conjunct Uranus' talent for the unexpected may trigger surprising results. Watch your step and don't be shocked if the news reflects odd events over the days before and after the Conjunction. Taureans should be especially careful.

(G) Mars leaves patient, plodding Taurus for impatient Gemini the day before the Full Moon, so its amazing talent for distraction will create plenty of opportunities for expressing that quality. Good for Aries and Gemini.

(H) This eventful and energizing Full Moon is packed with transits that affect multiple days before and after. The Venus Jupiter Sextile with the Aquarius Full Moon makes this perfect for connecting with your group, so get out of the house and enjoy your community. Good for Capricorn and Aquarius.

(I) As the Sun enters heart-based Leo, a wonderful synergy connects the Sun, Venus, Mars and Jupiter, encouraging socializing and bravery in matters of the heart. A wonderful time to start a relationship or infuse a current one with passion. Excellent for the Fire and Air Signs.

(J) As Mercury enters its Ruling Feminine Sign Virgo, it passes over the heart of the Lion, the Royal Star Regulus, which will be triggered multiple times by transits in the coming weeks. This is a wonderful time to speak from the heart, even while using that highly organized planetary position to create order in your life. Great for the Earth Signs, especially Virgo.

Mercury☿ 27° Cancer♋ enters Leo♌ on the 2nd at 5:49am,
enters Virgo♍ on the 25th at 3:41pm.
Venus♀ 17° Cancer♋ enters Leo♌ on the 11th at 9:18am.
Mars♂ 16° Taurus♉ enters Gemini on the 20th at 1:42pm.
Jupiter♃ 8° Gemini. Saturn♄ Rx 19° Pisces♓.
Uranus♅ 25° Taurus♉.
Neptune♆ 29° Pisces♓ turns Rx on the 2nd at 3:40am at 29°.
Pluto♇ Rx 01° Aquarius♒.

Signs

♈ Aries Begins
♉ Taurus Owns
♊ Gemini Engages
♋ Cancer Nurtures
♌ Leo Embraces
♍ Virgo Improves
♎ Libra Commits
♏ Scorpio Manages
♐ Sagittarius Views
♑ Capricorn Climbs
♒ Aquarius Herds
♓ Pisces Dreams

Planets

☉ Sun Spirit
☽ Moon Emotes
☿ Mercury Thinks
♀ Venus Feels
♂ Mars Acts
♃ Jupiter Expands
♄ Saturn Contracts
♅ Uranus Disrupts
♆ Neptune Envisions
♇ ⯓ Pluto Unearths

Aspects

☌ Conjunct 0° Aligns
∥ Parallel 0° Equals
⚹ Sextile 60° Helps
□ Square 90° Works
△ Trine 120° Supports
☍ Opposition 180° Counters

JULY 2024

Sunday	Monday	Tuesday
	♅♂♀♄♃☿ ☽♉ 1	☿ Enters ♌ 5:49am ♅♀♆☿♇ A ☽♊ 2 ♀△♄ ☿△♆ ☉∥☽ ♆Rx 8:49am 8:42am - 8:49am
☿♀♃♃ ☽♌ 7 ☉∥☽	Muharram C ☽♌ 8 ☿ ☿⚹♃ ☿∥♅ ♀⚹♅ ♂ ♅ 11:03pm	☽♍ 9 6:47am 6:47am
Bastille Day ☽♏ 14 ☉∥♃ 7:52am ♇♀ 7:52am	F ♄ ☽♏ 15 ♂☌♅ ☿	♇♆♇ ☽♐ 16 ☉△☽ 6:24pm ♅♂ 6:10pm - 6:24pm
Full ☽ 3:16am 29° ♑ H ♆♂♇♇ ☽♒ 21 ♂△♇ ☉△♆ ♀⚹♃ ☉☍☽ ☿□♅ 4:42am 4:26am - 4:42am	☉ Enters ♌ 12:44am I ♃ ☽♒ 22 ☉☍♇ ♀	☽♓ 23 ☉∥♂ 6:22am ♅☿♂ 2:57am - 6:22am
Delta Aquarid Meteors ♅♄♂ ☽♉ 28 ☉∥☽ ♀	♃♅♆♇ ☽♊ 29 2:27pm ☿ 1:59pm - 2:27pm	♂♃ ☽♊ 30 ☉⚹☽ ♄

All calculations are Pacific Clock Time (PST & PDT)

Cancer the Crab to Leo the Lion

Wednesday	Thursday	Friday	Saturday
♃ ☽♊ 3 ☉∥♀ ☿☍♇ ♄	Independence Day ☽♋ 4 ☿∥♃ 1:51pm ♆ 1:43pm - 1:51pm	New ☽ 3:57pm 14° ♋ B ☽♋ 5 ☉☌☽ ♂⚹♄	♄♂♀♅♆ ☽♌ 6 8:55pm ♇ 8:47pm - 8:55pm
D ☽♍ 10 ☉⚹☽ ☉△♄ ☿∥♂ ♃♄	♀ Enters ♌ 9:18am E ♂♅♀♇ ♀∥♃ ♀△♆ ☽♎ 11 7:06pm ♆ 6:54pm - 7:06pm	♆♃ ☽♎ 12 ♀☍♇	1st Quarter ☽ 3:48pm ♄☿ ☽♎ 13 ☉□☽ 3:48pm --------
♀ ☽♐ 17 ♃	☿ ☽♐ 18 ♂∥♅ ☉⚹♅ ♄	☽♑ 19 ♀∥♅ ♀∥♂ 1:13am ♆ 12:58am - 1:13am	♂ Enters ♊ 1:42pm G ♄♅ ☽♑ 20 ♂⚹♆
♄♄ ☽♓ 24 ♃	☿ Enters ♍ 3:41pm J ♅♆♆♇♂ ☽♈ 25 ☉⚹♂ ☉△☽ 7:52am 7:31am - 7:52am	♃♀☿ ☽♈ 26 ☉∥♅ 3:14pm --------	3rd Quarter ☽ 7:51pm ☿♀ ☽♉ 27 ☉□☽ 10:22am ♇ -------- 10:22am
♀ ☽♋ 31 8:18pm ♆ 7:46pm - 8:18pm	**Notes**		

Add 1 Hour for Mountain Time (MT)) Add 2 Hours for Central Time (CT) Add 3 Hours for Eastern Time (ET)

August Forecast

August starts off so well and then, on the 4th at the New Moon, Venus changes Sign while Mercury turns Retrograde, setting the theme for the rest of the month that is a little slower and more considered than the rush of months leading up to this. There are bumps to watch for, especially the Full Moon on the 19th in the last degrees of Leo.

(A) The New Moon at 12 degrees of Leo occurs while Venus is passing over the Royal Star Regulus, the heart of the Lion, just as Mercury turns Direct in Virgo. That is a rough Sign for a Mercury Retrograde because it normally works so well. Until the 28th when Mercury turns Direct, double check any details. Venus passing over Regulus opens the door for making connections with others related to healing. To minimize the turbulence, avoid planning too much on this day.
(B) A good day for tasks requiring precision and communication. Jupiter Sextile the Sun offers local opportunities. Be optimistic! Good for Leo and Gemini.
(C) Mercury Retrogrades into Leo, so stop cleaning the closets and go to the beach. Mars Conjunct Jupiter wants you to get up and out, especially you Air Signs.
(D) We hope you took advantage of yesterday's easy Aspects because this day is about arduous work. Be prepared to resolve disagreements to accomplish your goals. Hardest for Gemini and Pisces.
(E) Expect static and discord, it will take extra effort and an abundance of charm to make events work out. Mercury Ruled Signs, Gemini and Virgo; your skills are needed!
(F) It's rare to see such a challenging Full Moon, but this one is happening late in the Sign and it brings together numerous conflicting

players, although it will be expressed in the outer world more than in the personal. Watch out for economic shifts and technology challenges due to the Sun Square Uranus. Leo and Taurus, watch out.
(G) The Sun enters Virgo hand in hand with the mission focused asteroid Vesta, the eternal flame. This infuses these days with a sense of mission and heat. The Sun's annual transit of the Lion's Heart, Regulus, is a passionate time. Focus on what imbues your life with joy. Great for the Earth Signs.
(H) This highly productive day is marred only by a Void of Course Moon. Make a list of tasks to follow and check them off as the day proceeds.
(I) Mercury turns Direct in the depths of Leo, so it will traverse Regulus again and give us another shot of joy when it does. Good for the Mercury Ruled Signs, Gemini and Virgo.
(J) Venus enters its highly social, Masculine Ruling Sign Libra, so use that to make the possibilities and the limits of your partnerships clear. Wonderful for the Air Signs.

Mercury☿ 3° Virgo♍ turns Rx on the 4th at 4° Virgo♍ at 9:55pm, enters Leo♌ on the 14th at 5:15pm, turns Direct on the 28th at 21° Leo♌ at 2:13pm.
Venus♀ 25° Leo♌ enters Virgo♍ on the 4th at 7:22pm, enters Libra♎ on the 29th at 6:22am.
Mars♂ 7° Gemini♊. Jupiter♃ 14° Gemini♊.
Saturn♄ Rx 18° Pisces♓.
Uranus♅ 26° Taurus♉.
Neptune♆ Rx 29° Pisces♓.
Pluto♇ Rx 00° Aquarius♒.

Signs

- ♈ Aries Begins
- ♉ Taurus Owns
- ♊ Gemini Engages
- ♋ Cancer Nurtures
- ♌ Leo Embraces
- ♍ Virgo Improves
- ♎ Libra Commits
- ♏ Scorpio Manages
- ♐ Sagittarius Views
- ♑ Capricorn Climbs
- ♒ Aquarius Herds
- ♓ Pluto Unearths

Planets

- ☉ Sun Spirit
- ☽ Moon Emotes
- ☿ Mercury Thinks
- ♀ Venus Feels
- ♂ Mars Acts
- ♃ Jupiter Expands
- ♄ Saturn Contracts
- ♅ Uranus Disrupts
- ♆ Neptune Envisions
- ♇ Pluto Unearths

Aspects

- ☌ Conjunct 0° Aligns
- ∥ Parallel 0° Equals
- ⚹ Sextile 60° Helps
- □ Square 90° Works
- △ Trine 120° Supports
- ☍ Opposition 180° Counters

AUGUST 2024

Sunday	Monday	Tuesday
Notes		
New ☽ 4:12am 12° ♌ ♀ Enters ♍ 7:22pm A ♂♃♅ ☽♌ **4** ☉☌☽ ☿Rx	♀☿♀ ☽♍ **5** ☉∥☽ 2:16pm ♅ 8:15am - 2:16pm	☽♍ **6** ♂♃
♀ ☽♏ **11**	1st Quarter ☽ 8:18am Tisha B'Av ♄♇ ☽♏ **12** ☉□☽ ♅	Lefthander's Day Perseid Meteors ♆♇ ☽♐ **13** 3:00am ☿ 2:00am - 3:00am
E ♇♃♂ ☽♒ **18** ☉☌☿ ☿□♅ ♀□♃	Full ☽ 11:25am 27° ♒ Raksha Bandhan F ☽♓ **19** ♀☍♄ ☉□♅ ☉☍☽ 3:51pm ☿♅ ♃□♄ 11:25am - 3:51pm	♄♄ ☽♓ **20** ♃♀
♃♀♂♅♆♇ ☽♊ **25** 8:03pm ☿ 6:40pm - 8:03pm	3rd Quarter ☽ 2:25am ☽♊ **26** ☉□☽	♃☿♂ ☽♊ **27** ♀△♅ ♄♀

All calculations are Pacific Clock Time (PST & PDT)

Leo the Lion to Virgo the Virgin

Wednesday	Thursday	Friday	Saturday
	☿ ☽♋ 1	♄♅ ☽♋ 2 ♀□♅	♆♂♃ ☽♌ 3 4:09am ♇ 3:31am - 4:09am
B ☿♅ ☿☌♀ ☽♍ 7 ☉⚹♃ ♄	♇ ☽♎ 8 2:31am ♆ 1:39am - 2:31am	♂♄♃ ☽♎ 9 ☉⚹☽ 2:44pm ----------	☿ ☽♏ 10 ♂∥♃ 3:33pm ♇ ---------- 3:33pm
☿ Enters ♌ 5:15pm C ☉△☽ ☽♐ 14 ♂☌♃ ♀♃♂♄	D ☿ ☽♑ 15 ♂□♄ 10:50am ♆ 9:51am - 10:50am	♀♄ ☽♑ 16 ☿∥♀	♅♆♇ ☽♒ 17 2:44pm 1:43pm -2:44pm
♅♆♆♇ ☽♈ 21 4:01pm ♂ 2:53pm - 4:01pm	☉ Enters ♍ 7:54am G ♀♃ ☽♈ 22 ♀□♂	☿⚹♂ H ♂☿☿ ☉△☽ ☽♉ 23 ☉∥☽ 5:00pm ♇ 5:44am - 5:00pm	♅♄ ☽♉ 24 ☉∥☿
I ☿'D' ☽♋ 28 ☉⚹☽ ♀☍♆ 1:47am ♆ 12:13am - 1:47am	♀ Enters ♎ 6:22am J ♄ ☽♋ 29 ♀△♇	♅♆♀♂ ☽♌ 30 10:09am ♇ 8:24am - 10:09am	♃♅♃ ☽♌ 31

Add 1 Hour for Mountain Time (MT)) Add 2 Hours for Central Time (CT) Add 3 Hours for Eastern Time (ET)

September Forecast

Boom! The month starts with a one two punch, followed by an uppercut! If you get the idea that this is a month to stay on your toes, you are correct! A fourth planet turns Retrograde joining the Outers and **the year's third Eclipse happens on the 17th.** At the beginning of the year, the Planets were bunched together but now the personal planets are on one side and the outer planets are on the other, with Jupiter and Mars in between. This gives a sense that worldly affairs are happening 'over there' someplace, and the allies we need are closer to home.

(A) Pluto backs into Capricorn as Uranus turns Retrograde, increasing the sense of worldly affairs being stalled.

(B) The New Moon encourages us to complete those projects that are part of our mission. Good for the Earth Signs.

(C) Mars leaves impatient Gemini for home building Cancer so do home improvement projects between now and the beginning of November for the best results. Great for the Water Signs. Cancer, watch out for acting impulsively.

(D) Saturn opposing the Sun subdues the solar energy and suppresses life cycles. Not a great time to starts things, especially for Gemini, Virgo, Sagittarius and Pisces.

(E) Mercury reenters its feminine Ruling Sign Virgo, easing communication and the nervous system. Practical tasks done by hand, organization and healing get an extra boost. Good for the Earth Signs.

(F) Powerful Venus Trines expansive Jupiter providing multiple opportunities to improve relationships on the days around this date, especially for the Air Signs.

(G) Pisces and Virgo will deeply feel the Partial Lunar Eclipse at the Full Moon. This Eclipse ties together Mercury, Saturn, Neptune and

Pluto, in the people focused Mutable Signs, part of a recurring theme seen in the ongoing Jupiter Saturn Square. This Square manifests in the crisis where young populations and businesses (Jupiter in Gemini) are living in coastal areas (Saturn in Pisces), being impacted by climate change. The period up to the second Eclipse on October 2nd will be emotionally complicated. Be kind to yourself and others.
(H) A highly social day that may spark lively discussions.

(I) As the Sun enters its Fall position of Libra at the Fall Equinox, Venus, the Ruler of Libra, enters Scorpio, the feminine Ruling Sign of Mars. Also, the Sun is Trine the waning Moon in Cancer in the early morning. There is an implicit feminine power at this time with the need to be deeply connected, that will endure until the middle of next month when Venus enters Sagittarius. Significant for Libra and Scorpio.
(J) Fast moving Mercury enters Libra, a Sign that loves to negotiate and periodically argue, so be willing to sacrifice efficiency for the sake of cooperation. Good for the Air Signs.
(K) In the time between eclipses even the Mars Trine Saturn Aspects can be welcome, so put your physical energy into something that will endure.

Mercury☿ 22° Leo♌ enters Virgo♍ on the 8th at 11:49pm, enters Libra♎ on the 26th at 1:08am.
Venus♀ 3° Libra♎ enters Scorpio♏ on the 22nd at 7:35pm.
Mars♂ 27° Gemini♊ enters Cancer♋ on the 4th at 12:46pm.
Jupiter♃ 19° Gemini♊. Saturn♄ Rx 16° Pisces♓.
Uranus♅ 27° Taurus♉ turns Rx on the 1st at 8:17am.
Neptune♆ Rx 29° Pisces♓.
Pluto♇ Rx 00° Aquarius♒ enters Capricorn♑ on the 1st at 5:07pm.

Signs

♈ Aries Begins
♉ Taurus Owns
♊ Gemini Engages
♋ Cancer Nurtures
♌ Leo Embraces
♍ Virgo Improves
♎ Libra Commits
♏ Scorpio Manages
♐ Sagittarius Views
♑ Capricorn Climbs
♒ Aquarius Herds
♓ Pisces Dreams

Planets

☉ Sun Spirit
☽ Moon Emotes
☿ Mercury Thinks
♀ Venus Feels
♂ Mars Acts
♃ Jupiter Expands
♄ Saturn Contracts
♅ Uranus Disrupts
♆ Neptune Envisions
♇ ⯓ Pluto Unearths

Aspects

☌ Conjunct 0° Aligns
∥ Parallel 0° Equals
⚹ Sextile 60° Helps
□ Square 90° Works
△ Trine 120° Supports
☍ Opposition 180° Counters

SEPTEMBER 2024

Sunday	Monday	Tuesday
♇ Enters ♑ 5:07am A ☿♂ ☽♍ 1 ♅Rx 8:48pm ♅ 5:24pm - 8:48pm	New ☽ 6:55pm 11° ♍ Labor Day B ☿ ☽♍ 2 ☉☌☽ ♂□♆	☽♍ 3 ♀∥♆ ☉∥☽ ♃♄
☿ Enters ♍ 11:49pm Grandparents Day E ♄ ☽♏ 8 ☉⚹☽	California Admission Day ♇♆♇ ☽♐ 9 10:25am ♅☿ 10:11am - 10:25am	1st Quarter ☽ 11:05pm ♀ ☽♐ 10 ☉□☽ ♄
♃♀ ☽♒ 15 ♀∥♄ ♅ 10:03pm --------	The Prophet's Birthday ♂♀ ☽♓ 16 2:38am ☿ -------- 2:38am	Full ☽ 7:34pm 25° ♓ Partial ☾ Eclipse G ♄♄♅♆ ☽♓ 17 ☉☍☽ ♃ Constitution Day
☉ Enters ♎ 5:43am ♀ Enters ♏ 7:35pm I ♆♇ ☽♊ 22 ☉△☽ ♀□♇ 3:24am Fall Equinox 3:13am - 3:24am	♃ ☽♊ 23 ♄	3rd Quarter ☽ 11:49am ♀ ☽♋ 24 ☿△♅ ☉□☽ 7:49am ☿♆ 4:58am - 7:49am
K ♀ ☽♍ 29 ♂△♄ 2:41am -------- 2:41am	♂ ☽♍ 30 ☉☌☿ ☿∥♆ ♄♃	

All calculations are Pacific Clock Time (PST & PDT)

Virgo the Virgin to Libra the Scales

Wednesday	Thursday	Friday	Saturday
♂ Enters ♋ 12:46pm C ♅♇♀ ☽♎ 4 9:11am ♆♂ 9:06am - 9:11am	♀♄ ☽♎ 5	Ganesh Chaturthi ♃☿ ☽♏ 6 ☿□♅ 10:18pm ♇ 10:08pm - 10:18pm	D ♂ ☽♏ 7 ☉☍♄
☽♑ 11 ☿⚹♂ 7:37pm ♃♆ 5:20pm - 7:37pm	☿♄ ☽♑ 12 ☉□♃ ♂	♅♆ ☽♑ 13 ☉△☽ ♀	F ♇♇ ☽♒ 14 ♀△♃ 12:53am 12:34am - 12:53am
♆♇ ☽♈ 18 ☉∥☽ ☿☍♄ 2:23am ♂ 2:02am - 2:23am	☿♃ ☽♈ 19 ☉△♅ ♀	♂ ☽♉ 20 ☉☍♆ 2:02am ♇ 1:38am - 2:02am	H ♅♄☿♃♂♅ ☽♉ 21 ☉△♇ ☿□♃
♂♄ ☽♋ 25 ☿△♇ ☿☍♆	☿ Enters ♎ 1:08am J ♅♆☿ ☽♌ 26 3:47pm ♇ 3:12pm - 3:47pm	♂♃ ☉∥♆ ☉⚹☽ ☽♌ 27 ♀	♃ ☽♌ 28 ♅ 8:35pm

Notes

Add 1 Hour for Mountain Time (MT)) Add 2 Hours for Central Time (CT) Add 3 Hours for Eastern Time (ET)

October Forecast

The month begins with the New Moon Eclipse, completing the cycle started on September 17th. After this deeply grounding day, the emotional and physical pressure will decrease. By the following Full Moon, people will feel mostly normal. With Jupiter turning Retrograde, all the Outer Planets are back tracking, so world events will seem to slow to a crawl. But the personal Planets are clipping along with our personal lives. Watch the news less and concentrate on your own happiness more.

(A) This Eclipse is about relationships, partnerships and families. It's time to accept new relationship paradigms that recognize that polarity is about souls more than bodies, which allows people to transcend traditional roles in the creation of their homes and families. This is a challenging time for Aries, Libra, Cancer & Capricorn.

(B) An abundance of supportive Aspects makes this a good day for any task where you don't want to encounter resistance. Good for the Fire and Air Signs.

(C) Jupiter turns Retrograde while supporting the Sun, Mercury and the marriage asteroid, Juno. Possibly reevaluate how your relationships have been operating and see if there is room for improvement.

(D) While the other Outer Planets continue to Retrograde, Pluto turns Direct. A deep undercurrent is washing away the remnants of outmoded systems in preparation for newer methods of global connection and communication that will be evident as Pluto transits Aquarius.

(E) A fast-moving Mercury plunges into the depths of Scorpio so think strategically about how to improve your personal tribe's power and wealth. That's what Scorpio does! The Sun Trine Jupiter will help that process. Great for the Water Signs.

(F) With so many conflicting Aspects among challenging Planets, tread carefully in your interactions today. (G) A great day to get things done but start early because the supportive Aspects are in the morning before the Moon changes Sign.

(H) This is a highly energized Full Moon with the Sun Conjunct Spica, the brightest Star in Virgo, the 'Great Goddess'. This is a highly productive, feminine archetype. Meanwhile, the Aries Moon defers to Mars in deeply feminine Cancer and Venus enters far-seeing Sagittarius. The message for women is to plan your path ahead cooperatively with optimism and energy.

(I) Whatever you do this day you will have the wind at your back and no obstructions ahead.

(J) The Sun enters Scorpio, gaining the help of Saturn and Mars for the next thirty days. Start tasks that require energy and discipline, and they will yield reliable results. Good for the Water Signs.

(K) This is a highly inventive day, but watch out that your experiments don't blow up!

(L) On this very social day you can get a great deal done as long as you follow your dreams and use your good taste.

•••

Mercury☿ 8° Libra♎ enters Scorpio♏ on the 13th at 12:23pm.

Venus♀ 9° Scorpio♏ enters Sagittarius♐ on the 17th at 12:28pm.

Mars♂ 15° Cancer♋.

Jupiter♃ 21° Gemini♊ turns Rx on the 9th at 12:04am.

Saturn♄ Rx 14° Pisces♓.

Uranus♅ Rx 26° Taurus♉.

Neptune♆ Rx 28 Pisces♓.

Pluto♇ Rx 29° Capricorn♑ turns Direct on the 11th
at 5:31pm at 29° Capricorn♑.

Signs

♈ Aries Begins
♉ Taurus Owns
♊ Gemini Engages
♋ Cancer Nurtures
♌ Leo Embraces
♍ Virgo Improves
♎ Libra Commits
♏ Scorpio Manages
♐ Sagittarius Views
♑ Capricorn Climbs
♒ Aquarius Herds
♓ Pisces Dreams

Planets

☉ Sun Spirit
☽ Moon Emotes
☿ Mercury Thinks
♀ Venus Feels
♂ Mars Acts
♃ Jupiter Expands
♄ Saturn Contracts
♅ Uranus Disrupts
♆ Neptune Envisions
♇ ⯓ Pluto Unearths

Aspects

☌ Conjunct 0° Aligns
∥ Parallel 0° Equals
⚹ Sextile 60° Helps
□ Square 90° Works
△ Trine 120° Supports
☍ Opposition 180° Counters

OCTOBER 2024

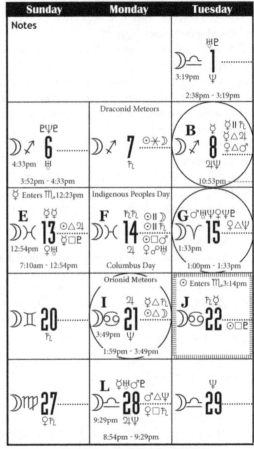

Sunday	Monday	Tuesday
Notes		♅♇ ☽♎ 1 3:19pm ♆ 2:38pm - 3:19pm
♇♆♇ ☽♐ 6 4:33pm ♅ 3:52pm - 4:33pm	Draconid Meteors ☽♐ 7 ☉⚹☽ ♄	B ☿ ☿∥♄ ☿△♃ ☽♐ 8 ♀△♂ ♃♆ 10:53pm
☿ Enters ♏ 12:23pm E ☿☿ ☽♓ 13 ☉△♃ ☿□♇ 12:54pm ♀♅ 7:10am - 12:54pm	Indigenous Peoples Day F ♄♄ ☉∥☽ ☽♓ 14 ☉∥♄ ☉□♂ ♃ ♀☍♅ Columbus Day	G ♂♅♆♀♆♇ ☽♈ 15 ♀△♆ 1:33pm 1:00pm - 1:33pm
☽♊ 20 ♄	Orionid Meteors I ♃ ☿△♄ ☉△☽ ☽♋ 21 3:49pm ♆ 1:59pm - 3:49pm	☉ Enters ♏ 3:14pm J ♄☿ ☽♋ 22 ☉□♇
☽♍ 27 ♀♄	L ☿♅♂♇ ☽♎ 28 ♂△♆ ♀□♄ 9:29pm ♃♆ 8:54pm - 9:29pm	♆ ☽♎ 29

All calculations are Pacific Clock Time (PST & PDT)

Libra the Scales to Scorpio the Scorpion

Wednesday	Thursday	Friday	Saturday
New ☽ 11:49am 10° ♎ Annular ☉ Eclipse **A** ♆☿☿ ☉☌☽ ☉∥☽ ☽♎ **2** ♂	Rosh Hashanah ♄♃ ☽♎ **3** ☉∥☿ Navratri	♀ ☽♏ **4** ♀△♄ 4:22am ♇ 3:40am - 4:22am	♄♀♂ ☽♏ **5** ☿□♂
C ☽♑ **9** ♃Rx 2:38am ---------- 2:38am	1st Quarter ☽ 11:54am ♄♀ ☽♑ **10** ☉□☽ ♂	**D** ♅♆♇♇ ☽♒ **11** ♇'D' 9:30am ☿ 8:52am - 9:30am	Yom Kippur ♀♃ ☽♒ **12** ☉△☽ Dussehra
Sukkot Begins Sundown ♃ ☽♈ **16**	Full ☽ 4:26am 24° ♈ ♀ Enters ♐ 12:28pm **H** ♀⚹♇ ♂∥♃ ☉☍☽ ☽♉ **17** 12:59pm ♂♇ 12:26pm - 12:59pm	♄♅ ☽♉ **18** ☿	♂♃♂♅♆♇ ☽♊ **19** 1:06pm ♀ 12:33pm - 1:06pm
Sukkot Ends ♂♅♆ ☽♌ **23** 10:23pm ♇ 9:47pm - 10:23pm	3rd Quarter ☽ 1:02am Shemini Atzeret **K** ♀♃♂ ☽♌ **24** ♂⚹♅ ☉□☽	Simchat Torah ♅♃ ☽♌ **25** ♀∥♇ ☿	☽♍ **26** ☉⚹☽ 8:47am ♅ 1:03am - 8:47am
♀♄♃ ☽♎ **30** ☿☍♅	Halloween Diwali ☿△♆ ☉∥☽ ☽♏ **31** 10:29am ♂♇ 9:56am - 10:29am	**Notes** *It's not too early to order your 2025 Planetary Calendar!*	

Add 1 Hour for Mountain Time (MT)) Add 2 Hours for Central Time (CT) Add 3 Hours for Eastern Time (ET)

November Forecast

The month starts out turbulent but then settles down. In the first full week, expect to see overblown egos, not surprisingly with the election happening. Saturn will turn Direct and Pluto will enter Aquarius, so big shifts happen. The Election Day has a very feminine, restrained chart, with the Sun supported by Saturn, promoting the power of mature women. We'll cover this in the expanded online video forecast.

(A) At the New Moon, the Planets are spread out so multiple themes are running concurrently. Scorpios, make time for yourself.

(B) Mercury enters Sagittarius, a position found in the charts of many great Astrologers, because they can see the big picture and connect the dots while also having a great sense of humor, so laugh more!
Mercury is slowing and turning Retrograde on the 25th, spending the rest of 2024 in the Sign of the Archer. Good for the Fire Signs, but hard for Geminis.

(C) Mars enters dramatic Leo so if people get noisy, blame it on that. Good for the Fire Signs who should be more expressive in their physical actions.
(D) Venus enters Capricorn, the Sign of the mature woman, bringing seriousness to personal relationships. Capricorns will feel more attractive.

(E) The Full Moon at the Star Algol engages numerous planets for a social time while Saturn turns Direct. The message? Compassion for others is a building block of a healthy society.

(F) As Pluto enters Aquarius, the Water Bearer, as it relates to irrigation, will begin to transform farming on the land and in the ocean.

(G) A good day for events that you want to go smoothly.
(H) The Sun enters optimistic and far-seeing Sagittarius, a good time for considering how your year has gone and how that can support your future plans. Great for the Fire Signs planning the future.
(I) Slowing Mercury turns Retrograde, complicating communications. Fortunately, the Retrograde in Sagittarius is typically not as difficult a transit as some, although you should double check the details when it matters, and don't expect emails to get through the first time.

(J) The second New Moon of the Month takes place at 9 degrees Sagittarius, Conjunct the warlike red Star Antares, the heart of the Scorpion. When Planets contact Antares, it plays out in society.
Having the New Moon there is a bit worrisome, but it shouldn't concern you too personally, unless you, or someone close to you, has personal Planets there in their birth chart. In which case, stay cool! We'll see how it plays out in society in the first week of December.

Mercury☿ 27° Scorpio♏ enters Sagittarius♐ on the 2nd at 12:17pm, turns Rx on the 25th at 22° Sagittarius♐ at 6:42pm.
Venus♀ 17° Sagittarius♐ enters Capricorn♑ on the 11th at 10:25am.
Mars♂ 28° Cancer♋ enters Leo♌ on the 3rd at 8:09pm.
Jupiter♃ Rx 20° Gemini♊.
Saturn♄ Rx 12° Pisces♓ turns Direct on the 15th.
Uranus♅ Rx 25° Taurus♉. Neptune Rx 27 Pisces♓.
Pluto♇ 29° Capricorn♑ 29° enters Aquarius♒ on the 19th at 12:29pm.

Signs

♈ Aries Begins
♉ Taurus Owns
♊ Gemini Engages
♋ Cancer Nurtures
♌ Leo Embraces
♍ Virgo Improves
♎ Libra Commits
♏ Scorpio Manages
♐ Sagittarius Views
♑ Capricorn Climbs
♒ Aquarius Herds
♓ Pisces Dreams

Planets

☉ Sun Spirit
☽ Moon Emotes
☿ Mercury Thinks
♀ Venus Feels
♂ Mars Acts
♃ Jupiter Expands
♄ Saturn Contracts
♅ Uranus Disrupts
♆ Neptune Envisions
♇ ♇ Pluto Unearths

Aspects

☌ Conjunct 0° Aligns
ll Parallel 0° Equals
⚹ Sextile 60° Helps
□ Square 90° Works
△ Trine 120° Supports
☍ Opposition 180° Counters

NOVEMBER 2024

Sunday	Monday	Tuesday
Notes	*It's not too early to order your 2025 Planetary Calendar!*	
♂ Enters ♌ 8:09pm Daylight Time Ends C ☽♐ **3** ♀ ♄ ♂☍♇ ♀☍♃	Taurid Meteors ☽♐ **4** ♀ ♃ ☉△♄	Election Day ☽♑ **5** 7:17am ♆ ☿ll♇ 2:23am - 7:17am
☽♓ **10** ♄♄ ☿	♀ Enters ♑ 10:25am Veterans Day D ☽♈ **11** ♅♆♆♇ ☉△☽ 10:25pm ♃♀ 10:13pm - 10:25pm	☽♈ **12** ♂☿ ☿□♄
Leonid Meteors ☽♊ **17** ♃ ☿♆ 8:08pm ----------	Leonid Meteors ☽♋ **18** ♄ ♀ ☉△♆ ☿ll♀ ☿☍♃ 12:49am ----------12:49am	♇ Enters ♒ 12:29pm F ☽♋ **19** ♅
☽♍ **24** ♅ ♃☿♆ 9:34pm ----------	I ☽♎ **25** ♇♂♆ ☉⚹☽ ☿Rx 3:19am ---------- 3:19am	☽♎ **26** ♃♄ ♀ ☿ll♀

All calculations are Pacific Clock Time (PST & PDT)

Scorpio the Scorpion to Sagittarius the Archer

Wednesday	Thursday	Friday	Saturday
Notes		New ☽ 5:46am 9° ♏ **A** ♄ ☽♏ 1 ☉☌☽	☿ Enters ♐ 12:17pm **B** ☿♇♆♂♇☿ ☽♐ 2 ☿⚹♇ ☿△♂ 10:19pm ♅ 9:50pm - 10:19pm
♄ ☽♑ 6 ☉⚹☽	♅♆♀♇☿ ☽♒ 7 2:57pm ♂ 2:37pm - 2:57pm	1st Quarter ☽ 9:55pm ♇☿ ☽♒ 8 ☉□☽	♃♀ ☽♓ 9 ☉∥☽ ♀□♆ 7:59pm ♅ 4:23pm - 7:59pm
♃ ☽♉ 13 10:58pm ♇ 10:49pm - 10:58pm	♀♄♅ ☽♉ 14 ♂	Full ☽ 1:28pm 24° ♉ **E** ♂♃♅♆♇ ☽♊ 15 ♄'D' ☉☍☽ 11:08pm 11:02pm - 11:08pm	♂ ☽♊ 16 ☉☍♅ ♄
G ♆♂♃ ☽♌ 20 ☉△☽ 5:50am ♇ 3:19am - 5:50am	☉ Enters ♐ 11:56am **H** ♂♃♅☿ ☽♌ 21 ☉⚹♇	3rd Quarter ☽ 5:27pm ☽♍ 22 ♀⚹♄ ☉□☽ 3:00pm ♅ 5:14am - 3:00pm	♀ ☽♍ 23 ♄
☿ ☽♏ 27 ☉△♂ 4:20pm ♇ 1:14am - 4:20pm	Thanksgiving Day ♄ ☽♏ 28 ♂	Black Friday ♀♇♆☿ ☽♏ 29 ☉∥☽ ♅ 10:18pm ----------	New ☽ 10:21pm 09° ♐ Small Business Saturday **J** ♀♇♂ ☽♐ 30 ☉☌☽ 3:52am ---------- 3:52am

Add 1 Hour for Mountain Time (MT)) Add 2 Hours for Central Time (CT) Add 3 Hours for Eastern Time (ET)

December Forecast

The first half of the month is a bit chaotic. Mercury is Retrograde, turning Direct at the Full Moon on the 15th. Mars, who does not like back tracking, turns Retrograde on the 6th as Venus enters Aquarius. Then the next day, Neptune turns Direct forming a loose Square in the people-focused, Mutable Signs, tying in Jupiter and Saturn. Expect the economy to still be working at cross purposes, while society focuses on human rights and daily needs.

(A) From the 4th through the 7th each day has significant Transits. On the 4th the big player is the Saturn Square the Sun, both in Jupiter Ruled Signs, showing the continuing concern about that which matters to people. Good for the Fire Signs.

(B) Venus, who does not turn Retrograde in 2024, enters socially conscious Aquarius. Connect with a wider circle of friends and community as the Winter Solstice approaches. Good for the Air Signs.

Mars turns Retrograde in fiery Leo, eventually backing into Cancer on January 6, 2025. Then turning Direct on February 24, 2025 and re-entering Leo in mid-April. Expect an extended period of frustrating, martial outbursts during the Retrograde. **Do your best to stay centered and grounded.** **(C)** Neptune turning Direct signals that global affairs, especially related to energy resources, are turning around. Good for Pisces. **(D)** This electric Full Moon connecting Jupiter and Mercury highlights mass media communications. Guard against overstimulation and information burnout. Mercury turning Direct in early Sagittarius adds an optimistic tone to the shortest days of the year. Good for the Fire and Air Signs. **(E)** Take advantage of this pair of Trines for any last-minute shopping, but watch for online technical glitches with Uranus Square the Moon.

(F) The Sun enters Capricorn. You may resent having to deny your own needs in favor of others, creating distance between people at a time when we traditionally come together. Consider ways in which your pride may be creating walls that prevent closeness in your relationships. This can be improved by going beyond any old hurts and forgiving all involved. **(G)** Christmas Eve is subject to a Jupiter Saturn Square, so don't expect the day to be easy. It's also complicated by a day long Void of Course Libra Moon. Try to get all your arrangements done in advance.

(H) The holidays are bunched together in the middle of the week, with the first day of Chanukah starting late after Christmas. The transits over the three days are mildly challenging, between the previous election and issues with the economy, expect discussions at get togethers to be polarized. Choose your guest list carefully and find ways to steer the conversations into lighter topics. The 26th has the most potential for conversational sparks. Be especially cautious when driving or walking in icy places.

(I) The New Moon in Capricorn highlights a continuing theme of strong, independent women and the importance of their collective wisdom to our families and societies, which we will need in 2025. ***Happy New Year!***

Mercury☿ Rx 20° Sagittarius♐ turns Direct on the 15th at 6° Sagittarius♐ at 12:56pm. Venus♀ 23° Capricorn♑ enters Aquarius♒ on the 6th at 10:13pm. Mars♂ 5° Leo♌ turns Rx on the 6th at 6° Leo at 3:32pm. Jupiter♃ Rx 17° Gemini♊. Saturn 12° Pisces♓. Uranus♅ Rx 24° Taurus♉. Neptune♆ Rx 27° Pisces♓ turns Direct on the 7th at 3:42pm. Pluto♇ 00° Aquarius♒.

Signs

♈ Aries Begins
♉ Taurus Owns
♊ Gemini Engages
♋ Cancer Nurtures
♌ Leo Embraces
♍ Virgo Improves
♎ Libra Commits
♏ Scorpio Manages
♐ Sagittarius Views
♑ Capricorn Climbs
♒ Aquarius Herds
♓ Pisces Dreams

Planets

☉ Sun Spirit
☽ Moon Emotes
☿ Mercury Thinks
♀ Venus Feels
♂ Mars Acts
♃ Jupiter Expands
♄ Saturn Contracts
♅ Uranus Disrupts
♆ Neptune Envisions
♇ ⯓ Pluto Unearths

Aspects

☌ Conjunct 0° Aligns
∥ Parallel 0° Equals
⚹ Sextile 60° Helps
□ Square 90° Works
△ Trine 120° Supports
☍ Opposition 180° Counters

DECEMBER 2024

Sunday	Monday	Tuesday
☿ ☽♐ **1** ♄♃	Cyber Monday ☽♑ **2** ♀△♅ 1:08pm ♆ 7:46am - 1:08pm	♄ ♀∥♇ ☽♑ **3** ☉∥☿
1st Quarter ☽ 7:26am ♄♅♆ ☽♓ **8** ☉□☽ ♃	♆♇♀♂☿ ☽♈ **9** 5:37am 12:44am - 5:37am	♃ ☽♈ **10** ☉△☽ 2:13pm ---------
Full ☽ 1:01am 23° ♊ D ☿'D' ☽♋ **15** ♂∥♃ ☉☍☽ 11:21am ♆ 6:31am - 11:21am	♄ ☽♋ **16**	♅♆ ☽♌ **17** 3:38pm ♇ 10:33am - 3:38pm
3rd Quarter ☽ 2:17pm Ursid Meteors ♇♂ ☽♎ **22** ☉□☽ 11:07am ♆ 5:26am - 11:07am	☿♃♄ ☽♎ **23**	Christmas Eve G ♀ ☽♎ **24** ♃□♄ 2:43am ---------
♀ ☽♑ **29** 8:37pm ♆ 3:34pm - 8:37pm	New ☽ 2:26pm 9° ♑ I ♄ ☉☌☽ ☽♑ **30** ☉∥♇	New Year's Eve ♅♆ ☽♑ **31**

All calculations are Pacific Clock Time (PST & PDT)

Sagittarius the Archer to Capricorn the Sea Goat

Wednesday	Thursday	Friday	Saturday
A ♅♆♀♇ ☽♒ **4** ♀⚹♆ ☿☍♃ ☉□♄ 8:20pm 3:33pm - 8:20pm	♇♀☿☿ ☽♒ **5** ☉⚹☽ ☉☌☿ ☉∥☽ ♂	♀ Enters ♒ 10:13pm St. Nicholas Day B ♃ ☽♒ **6** ☉∥♀ ♂Rx ♅ ☿□♄ 4:01pm ----------	C ♄ ♆'D' ☽♓ **7** ♀☌♇ ☉☍♃ 1:48am ☿ ---------- 1:48am
☽♉ **11** 7:54am ♇♀♂ -------- 7:54am	♅♄♂♃♅ ☽♉ **12** ☿⚹♀ ♀☍♂	Geminid Meteors ♆♇♂♀ ☽♊ **13** ☉∥♇ 9:21am ☿ 4:38am - 9:21am	Geminid Meteors ♃ ☽♊ **14** ♄
♂☿♂♃♃ ☽♌ **18** ☿∥♀ ☉□♆ ♀	E ☉△☽ ♀△♃ ☽♍ **19** 11:36pm ♅ 9:19pm - 11:36pm	☽♍ **20** ☿	☉ Enters ♑ 1:20am Winter Solstice F ♅ ☽♍ **21** ♄♃ Ursid Meteors
Christmas Day ♀ ☽♏ **25** ☉⚹☽ 12:06am ♇♂ -------- 12:06am	Chanukah (1st Day) Kwanzaa (1st Day) H ♄☿ ☽♏ **26** ☿☍♃ ♀♅ ☿□♄	♇♆♇♂ ☽♐ **27** ☉∥☽ ♀□♅ 11:46am 6:23am - 11:46am	☿ ☽♐ **28** ♃♄

Notes

It's Time to order your
2025 Planetary Calendar!

Add 1 Hour for Mountain Time (MT)) Add 2 Hours for Central Time (CT) Add 3 Hours for Eastern Time (ET)

JANUARY 2024

00:00 UT

Day	Sid.t	☉	☽	☿	♀	♂	♃	♄	♅	♆	♇	☊	Ω	⚸	⚷	Day
M 1	6 40 36	10♑ 2'20	6♍ 0	22°R17	2♐37	27♐19	5♉35	3♓15	19°R23	25♓ 5	29♑21	21°R 5	20♈53	9♍58	15♈28	M 1
T 2	6 44 33	11° 3'29	17°49	22°D11	3°50	28° 3	5°35	3°20	19♉22	25° 5	29°23	21♈ 0	20°49	10° 5	15°28	T 2
W 3	6 48 29	12° 4'38	29°37	22♐14	5° 3	28°48	5°36	3°25	19°20	25° 6	29°25	20°58	20°46	10°12	15°28	W 3
T 4	6 52 26	13° 5'47	11♎30	22°26	6°16	29°32	5°36	3°31	19°19	25° 7	29°27	20°D57	20°43	10°18	15°29	T 4
F 5	6 56 23	14° 6'56	23°33	22°46	7°29	0♑17	5°37	3°36	19°18	25° 8	29°29	20°R57	20°40	10°25	15°29	F 5
S 6	7 0 19	15° 8'06	5♏51	23°13	8°42	1° 1	5°38	3°42	19°17	25° 9	29°31	20°57	20°37	10°32	15°30	S 6
S 7	7 4 16	16° 9'16	18°31	23°46	9°56	1°46	5°40	3°48	19°16	25°10	29°33	20°54	20°34	10°38	15°30	S 7
M 8	7 8 12	17°10'26	1♐35	24°26	11° 9	2°31	5°41	3°53	19°15	25°11	29°35	20°49	20°30	10°45	15°31	M 8
T 9	7 12 9	18°11'36	15° 6	25°10	12°22	3°16	5°43	3°59	19°14	25°13	29°37	20°42	20°27	10°52	15°32	T 9
W10	7 16 5	19°12'46	29° 5	25°59	13°36	4° 1	5°45	4° 5	19°13	25°14	29°39	20°31	20°24	10°59	15°32	W10
T 11	7 20 2	20°13'56	13♑27	26°52	14°49	4°46	5°47	4°11	19°12	25°15	29°40	20°19	20°21	11° 5	15°33	T 11
F 12	7 23 58	21°15'06	28° 8	27°49	16° 3	5°31	5°50	4°17	19°11	25°16	29°42	20° 7	20°18	11°12	15°34	F 12
S 13	7 27 55	22°16'16	12♒59	28°49	17°16	6°16	5°52	4°23	19°11	25°17	29°44	19°55	20°15	11°19	15°35	S 13
S 14	7 31 52	23°17'25	27°51	29°52	18°30	7° 1	5°55	4°29	19°10	25°19	29°46	19°46	20°11	11°25	15°36	S 14
M15	7 35 48	24°18'33	12♓36	0♑58	19°43	7°46	5°58	4°35	19° 9	25°20	29°48	19°39	20° 8	11°32	15°37	M15
T 16	7 39 45	25°19'41	27° 7	2° 6	20°57	8°31	6° 1	4°41	19° 9	25°21	29°50	19°36	20° 5	11°39	15°38	T 16
W17	7 43 41	26°20'48	11♈22	3°17	22°10	9°16	6° 4	4°48	19° 8	25°23	29°52	19°34	20° 2	11°45	15°39	W17
T 18	7 47 38	27°21'54	25°18	4°29	23°24	10° 1	6° 8	4°54	19° 8	25°24	29°54	19°34	19°59	11°52	15°40	T 18
F 19	7 51 34	28°22'59	8♉57	5°43	24°38	10°46	6°12	5° 0	19° 7	25°25	29°56	19°34	19°55	11°59	15°42	F 19
S 20	7 55 31	29°24'04	22°20	6°59	25°51	11°32	6°15	5° 7	19° 7	25°27	29°58	19°32	19°52	12° 5	15°43	S 20
S 21	7 59 27	0♒25'08	5♊28	8°16	27° 5	12°17	6°20	5°13	19° 6	25°28	29°59	19°28	19°49	12°12	15°44	S 21
M22	8 3 24	1°26'11	18°24	9°35	28°19	13° 2	6°24	5°19	19° 6	25°30	0♒ 2	19°21	19°46	12°19	15°45	M22
T 23	8 7 21	2°27'13	1♋ 8	10°55	29°33	13°48	6°28	5°26	19° 6	25°31	0° 4	19°11	19°43	12°25	15°47	T 23
W24	8 11 17	3°28'14	13°42	12°16	0♑47	14°33	6°33	5°33	19° 6	25°33	0° 6	18°58	19°40	12°32	15°48	W24
T 25	8 15 14	4°29'14	26° 6	13°38	2° 1	15°18	6°38	5°39	19° 5	25°34	0° 8	18°44	19°36	12°39	15°50	T 25
F 26	8 19 10	5°30'14	8♌20	15° 1	3°14	16° 4	6°43	5°46	19° 5	25°36	0°10	18°31	19°33	12°45	15°52	F 26
S 27	8 23 7	6°31'13	20°26	16°25	4°28	16°49	6°48	5°52	19°D 5	25°38	0°12	18°18	19°30	12°52	15°53	S 27
S 28	8 27 3	7°32'10	2♍23	17°50	5°42	17°35	6°54	5°59	19° 5	25°39	0°14	18° 7	19°27	12°59	15°55	S 28
M29	8 31 0	8°33'07	14°15	19°16	6°56	18°20	6°59	6° 6	19° 5	25°41	0°15	17°59	19°24	13° 5	15°57	M29
T 30	8 34 56	9°34'04	26° 2	20°43	8°10	19° 6	7° 5	6°13	19° 5	25°43	0°17	17°54	19°20	13°12	15°58	T 30
W31	8 38 53	10♒34'59	7♎50	22♑10	9♑24	19♑52	7♉11	6♓20	19♉ 6	25♓44	0♒19	17♈52	19♈17	13♍19	16♈ 0	W31

Delta T = 69.10 sec

FEBRUARY 2024

00:00 UT

Day	Sid.t	☉	☽	☿	♀	♂	♃	♄	♅	♆	♇	☊	☊	⚸	⚷	Day
T 1	8 42 50	11♒35'54	19♎42	23♑39	10♑38	20♑37	7♉17	6♓26	19♉ 6	25♓46	0♒21	17°D51	19♈14	13♍25	16♈ 2	T 1
F 2	8 46 46	12°36'48	1♏42	25° 8	11°52	21°23	7°23	6°33	19° 6	25°48	0°23	17♈52	19°11	13°32	16° 4	F 2
S 3	8 50 43	13°37'41	13°58	26°38	13° 6	22° 9	7°30	6°40	19° 6	25°50	0°25	17°R52	19° 8	13°39	16° 6	S 3
S 4	8 54 39	14°38'34	26°33	28° 9	14°20	22°55	7°36	6°47	19° 7	25°51	0°27	17°51	19° 5	13°45	16° 8	S 4
M 5	8 58 36	15°39'26	9♐32	29°40	15°34	23°41	7°43	6°54	19° 7	25°53	0°29	17°49	19° 1	13°52	16°10	M 5
T 6	9 2 32	16°40'17	23° 0	1♒13	16°49	24°26	7°50	7° 1	19° 8	25°55	0°31	17°43	18°58	13°59	16°12	T 6
W 7	9 6 29	17°41'07	6♑58	2°46	18° 3	25°12	7°57	7° 8	19° 8	25°57	0°33	17°36	18°55	14° 5	16°14	W 7
T 8	9 10 25	18°41'56	21°24	4°19	19°17	25°58	8° 4	7°15	19° 9	25°59	0°35	17°27	18°52	14°12	16°16	T 8
F 9	9 14 22	19°42'44	6♒14	5°54	20°31	26°44	8°11	7°22	19°10	26° 1	0°36	17°18	18°49	14°19	16°19	F 9
S 10	9 18 19	20°43'31	21°19	7°30	21°45	27°30	8°19	7°29	19°10	26° 3	0°38	17° 9	18°46	14°25	16°21	S 10
S 11	9 22 15	21°44'16	6♓31	9° 6	22°59	28°16	8°27	7°37	19°11	26° 5	0°40	17° 1	18°42	14°32	16°23	S 11
M12	9 26 12	22°45'00	21°38	10°43	24°13	29° 2	8°35	7°44	19°12	26° 7	0°42	16°56	18°39	14°39	16°25	M12
T 13	9 30 8	23°45'42	6♈31	12°21	25°28	29°48	8°42	7°51	19°13	26° 9	0°44	16°54	18°36	14°45	16°28	T 13
W14	9 34 5	24°46'23	21° 5	13°59	26°42	0♒34	8°51	7°58	19°14	26°11	0°46	16°D54	18°33	14°52	16°30	W14
T 15	9 38 1	25°47'02	5♉15	15°39	27°56	1°21	8°59	8° 5	19°15	26°13	0°47	16°54	18°30	14°59	16°33	T 15
F 16	9 41 58	26°47'40	19° 1	17°19	29°10	2° 7	9° 7	8°13	19°16	26°15	0°49	16°55	18°26	15° 5	16°35	F 16
S 17	9 45 54	27°48'15	2♊24	19° 0	0♒24	2°53	9°16	8°20	19°17	26°17	0°51	16°R56	18°23	15°12	16°38	S 17
S 18	9 49 51	28°48'49	15°27	20°42	1°39	3°39	9°25	8°27	19°18	26°19	0°53	16°54	18°20	15°19	16°40	S 18
M19	9 53 48	29°49'22	28°12	22°25	2°53	4°25	9°33	8°34	19°19	26°21	0°55	16°50	18°17	15°25	16°43	M19
T 20	9 57 44	0♓49'52	10♋44	24° 9	4° 7	5°11	9°42	8°42	19°20	26°23	0°56	16°45	18°14	15°32	16°46	T 20
W21	10 1 41	1°50'21	23° 3	25°54	5°21	5°58	9°51	8°49	19°21	26°25	0°58	16°37	18°11	15°39	16°48	W21
T 22	10 5 37	2°50'48	5♌13	27°40	6°36	6°44	10° 1	8°56	19°23	26°27	1° 0	16°29	18° 7	15°45	16°51	T 22
F 23	10 9 34	3°51'13	17°15	29°27	7°50	7°30	10°10	9° 4	19°24	26°29	1° 1	16°20	18° 4	15°52	16°54	F 23
S 24	10 13 30	4°51'36	29°12	1♓14	9° 4	8°17	10°20	9°11	19°25	26°31	1° 3	16°12	18° 1	15°59	16°57	S 24
S 25	10 17 27	5°51'58	11♍ 3	3° 3	10°18	9° 3	10°29	9°18	19°27	26°34	1° 5	16° 6	17°58	16° 5	16°59	S 25
M26	10 21 23	6°52'18	22°52	4°52	11°33	9°49	10°39	9°25	19°28	26°36	1° 7	16° 1	17°55	16°12	17° 2	M26
T 27	10 25 20	7°52'36	4♎41	6°43	12°47	10°36	10°49	9°33	19°30	26°38	1° 8	15°59	17°52	16°19	17° 5	T 27
W28	10 29 17	8°52'53	16°31	8°34	14° 1	11°22	10°59	9°40	19°31	26°40	1°10	15°D58	17°48	16°25	17° 8	W28
T 29	10 33 13	9♓53'08	28♎26	10♓26	15♒15	12♒ 9	11♉ 9	9♓47	19♉33	26♓42	1♒11	15♈59	17♈45	16♍32	17♈11	T 29

Delta T = 69.09 sec

MARCH 2024

00:00 UT

Day	Sid.t	☉	☽	☿	♀	♂	♃	♄	♅	♆	♇	☊	Ω	⚸	⚷	Day
F 1	10 37 10	10♓53'22	10♏29	12♓19	16♒30	12♒55	11♉19	9♓55	19♉35	26♓44	1♒13	16♈ 0	17♈42	16♍39	17♈14	F 1
S 2	10 41 6	11°53'34	22°45	14°13	17°44	13°42	11°29	10° 2	19°36	26°47	1°15	16° 2	17°39	16°45	17°17	S 2
S 3	10 45 3	12°53'45	5♐18	16° 8	18°58	14°28	11°40	10° 9	19°38	26°49	1°16	16° 3	17°36	16°52	17°20	S 3
M 4	10 48 59	13°53'55	18°13	18° 3	20°12	15°15	11°50	10°17	19°40	26°51	1°18	16°R 3	17°32	16°59	17°23	M 4
T 5	10 52 56	14°54'02	1♑33	19°59	21°27	16° 1	12° 1	10°24	19°42	26°53	1°19	16° 2	17°29	17° 5	17°26	T 5
W 6	10 56 52	15°54'09	15°21	21°55	22°41	16°48	12°11	10°31	19°44	26°56	1°21	16° 0	17°26	17°12	17°29	W 6
T 7	11 0 49	16°54'13	29°37	23°52	23°55	17°34	12°22	10°39	19°46	26°58	1°22	15°56	17°23	17°19	17°32	T 7
F 8	11 4 46	17°54'16	14♒18	25°48	25°10	18°21	12°33	10°46	19°48	27° 0	1°24	15°52	17°20	17°25	17°36	F 8
S 9	11 8 42	18°54'18	29°20	27°45	26°24	19° 7	12°44	10°53	19°50	27° 2	1°25	15°48	17°17	17°32	17°39	S 9
S 10	11 12 39	19°54'17	14♓33	29°41	27°38	19°54	12°55	11° 1	19°52	27° 5	1°26	15°45	17°13	17°39	17°42	S 10
M11	11 16 35	20°54'15	29°48	1♈36	28°52	20°41	13° 7	11° 8	19°54	27° 7	1°28	15°43	17°10	17°45	17°45	M11
T 12	11 20 32	21°54'10	14♈54	3°30	0♓ 7	21°27	13°18	11°15	19°56	27° 9	1°29	15°D42	17° 7	17°52	17°48	T 12
W13	11 24 28	22°54'04	29°43	5°23	1°21	22°14	13°29	11°22	19°58	27°11	1°31	15°43	17° 4	17°59	17°52	W13
T 14	11 28 25	23°53'55	14♉ 9	7°13	2°35	23° 0	13°41	11°30	20° 1	27°14	1°32	15°44	17° 1	18° 5	17°55	T 14
F 15	11 32 21	24°53'44	28° 8	9° 2	3°49	23°47	13°52	11°37	20° 3	27°16	1°33	15°45	16°58	18°12	17°58	F 15
S 16	11 36 18	25°53'31	11♊41	10°48	5° 4	24°34	14° 4	11°44	20° 5	27°18	1°35	15°46	16°54	18°19	18° 2	S 16
S 17	11 40 15	26°53'16	24°49	12°31	6°18	25°20	14°16	11°51	20° 8	27°20	1°36	15°R47	16°51	18°25	18° 5	S 17
M18	11 44 11	27°52'59	7♋35	14°10	7°32	26° 7	14°28	11°58	20°10	27°23	1°37	15°47	16°48	18°32	18° 8	M18
T 19	11 48 8	28°52'39	20° 2	15°45	8°46	26°54	14°40	12° 5	20°12	27°25	1°38	15°46	16°45	18°39	18°12	T 19
W20	11 52 4	29°52'17	2♌15	17°15	10° 1	27°40	14°52	12°13	20°15	27°27	1°39	15°44	16°42	18°45	18°15	W20
T 21	11 56 1	0♈51'53	14°17	18°40	11°15	28°27	15° 4	12°20	20°17	27°30	1°41	15°42	16°38	18°52	18°19	T 21
F 22	11 59 57	1°51'26	26°12	20° 0	12°29	29°14	15°16	12°27	20°20	27°32	1°42	15°39	16°35	18°59	18°22	F 22
S 23	12 3 54	2°50'57	8♍ 2	21°14	13°43	0♓ 0	15°28	12°34	20°23	27°34	1°43	15°37	16°32	19° 5	18°25	S 23
S 24	12 7 50	3°50'27	19°51	22°22	14°58	0°47	15°40	12°41	20°25	27°36	1°44	15°36	16°29	19°12	18°29	S 24
M25	12 11 47	4°49'54	1♎40	23°23	16°12	1°34	15°53	12°48	20°28	27°39	1°45	15°35	16°26	19°19	18°32	M25
T 26	12 15 44	5°49'19	13°32	24°17	17°26	2°20	16° 5	12°55	20°30	27°41	1°46	15°D34	16°23	19°25	18°36	T 26
W27	12 19 40	6°48'41	25°28	25° 4	18°40	3° 7	16°18	13° 2	20°33	27°43	1°47	15°35	16°19	19°32	18°39	W27
T 28	12 23 37	7°48'03	7♏32	25°44	19°54	3°54	16°30	13° 9	20°36	27°45	1°48	15°35	16°16	19°39	18°43	T 28
F 29	12 27 33	8°47'22	19°45	26°17	21° 8	4°41	16°43	13°16	20°39	27°48	1°49	15°36	16°13	19°45	18°46	F 29
S 30	12 31 30	9°46'39	2♐ 9	26°42	22°23	5°27	16°56	13°22	20°41	27°50	1°50	15°36	16°10	19°52	18°50	S 30
S 31	12 35 26	10♈45'55	14♐49	27♈ 0	23♓37	6♓14	17♉ 8	13♓29	20♉44	27♓52	1♒51	15♈37	16♈ 7	19♍59	18♈53	S 31

Delta T = 69.08 sec

APRIL 2024 — 00:00 UT

Day	Sid.t	☉	☽	☿	♀	♂	♃	♄	♅	♆	♇	☊	☊	⚸	⚷	Day
M 1	12 39 23	11♈45'09	27♐46	27♈10	24♓51	7♓ 1	17♉21	13♓36	20♉47	27♓54	1♒52	15♈37	16♈ 3	20♍ 5	18♈57	M 1
T 2	12 43 19	12°44'21	11♑ 3	27°R13	26° 5	7°47	17°34	13°43	20°50	27°57	1°53	15°R37	16° 0	20°12	19° 0	T 2
W 3	12 47 16	13°43'31	24°42	27° 9	27°19	8°34	17°47	13°49	20°53	27°59	1°54	15°37	15°57	20°19	19° 4	W 3
T 4	12 51 13	14°42'40	8♒45	26°58	28°33	9°21	18° 0	13°56	20°56	28° 1	1°55	15°37	15°54	20°25	19° 7	T 4
F 5	12 55 9	15°41'46	23° 9	26°41	29°48	10° 7	18°13	14° 3	20°59	28° 3	1°55	15°D37	15°51	20°32	19°11	F 5
S 6	12 59 6	16°40'51	7♓53	26°18	1♈ 2	10°54	18°26	14° 9	21° 2	28° 5	1°56	15°37	15°48	20°39	19°15	S 6
S 7	13 3 2	17°39'55	22°51	25°49	2°16	11°41	18°39	14°16	21° 5	28° 8	1°57	15°37	15°44	20°45	19°18	S 7
M 8	13 6 59	18°38'56	7♈54	25°16	3°30	12°27	18°53	14°22	21° 8	28°10	1°58	15°R38	15°41	20°52	19°22	M 8
T 9	13 10 55	19°37'55	22°56	24°39	4°44	13°14	19° 6	14°29	21°11	28°12	1°58	15°38	15°38	20°59	19°25	T 9
W10	13 14 52	20°36'52	7♉46	23°58	5°58	14° 1	19°19	14°35	21°14	28°14	1°59	15°37	15°35	21° 5	19°29	W10
T 11	13 18 48	21°35'47	22°18	23°15	7°12	14°47	19°33	14°42	21°17	28°16	2° 0	15°37	15°32	21°12	19°32	T 11
F 12	13 22 45	22°34'41	6♊27	22°31	8°26	15°34	19°46	14°48	21°20	28°18	2° 0	15°36	15°29	21°19	19°36	F 12
S 13	13 26 42	23°33'32	20° 9	21°45	9°41	16°21	19°59	14°54	21°24	28°20	2° 1	15°35	15°25	21°25	19°39	S 13
S 14	13 30 38	24°32'20	3♋25	21° 0	10°55	17° 7	20°13	15° 1	21°27	28°23	2° 1	15°34	15°22	21°32	19°43	S 14
M15	13 34 35	25°31'07	16°16	20°16	12° 9	17°54	20°26	15° 7	21°30	28°25	2° 2	15°34	15°19	21°38	19°46	M15
T 16	13 38 31	26°29'51	28°46	19°34	13°23	18°40	20°40	15°13	21°33	28°27	2° 2	15°D34	15°16	21°45	19°50	T 16
W17	13 42 28	27°28'33	10♌59	18°54	14°37	19°27	20°54	15°19	21°36	28°29	2° 3	15°34	15°13	21°52	19°53	W17
T 18	13 46 24	28°27'12	22°59	18°17	15°51	20°13	21° 7	15°25	21°40	28°31	2° 3	15°35	15° 9	21°58	19°57	T 18
F 19	13 50 21	29°25'50	4♍51	17°44	17° 5	21° 0	21°21	15°31	21°43	28°33	2° 4	15°36	15° 6	22° 5	20° 1	F 19
S 20	13 54 17	0♉24'25	16°39	17°15	18°19	21°46	21°35	15°37	21°46	28°35	2° 4	15°37	15° 3	22°12	20° 4	S 20
S 21	13 58 14	1°22'58	28°27	16°50	19°33	22°33	21°48	15°43	21°49	28°37	2° 4	15°39	15° 0	22°18	20° 8	S 21
M22	14 2 10	2°21'29	10♎19	16°30	20°47	23°19	22° 2	15°49	21°53	28°39	2° 5	15°R39	14°57	22°25	20°11	M22
T 23	14 6 7	3°19'58	22°17	16°15	22° 1	24° 6	22°16	15°54	21°56	28°41	2° 5	15°39	14°54	22°32	20°14	T 23
W24	14 10 4	4°18'25	4♏24	16° 5	23°15	24°52	22°30	16° 0	21°59	28°43	2° 5	15°38	14°50	22°38	20°18	W24
T 25	14 14 0	5°16'51	16°41	16° 0	24°29	25°38	22°44	16° 6	22° 3	28°45	2° 5	15°36	14°47	22°45	20°21	T 25
F 26	14 17 57	6°15'14	29° 9	15°D59	25°43	26°25	22°58	16°11	22° 6	28°47	2° 6	15°34	14°44	22°52	20°25	F 26
S 27	14 21 53	7°13'36	11♐50	16° 4	26°57	27°11	23°11	16°17	22°10	28°48	2° 6	15°30	14°41	22°58	20°28	S 27
S 28	14 25 50	8°11'57	24°45	16°14	28°11	27°57	23°25	16°22	22°13	28°50	2° 6	15°27	14°38	23° 5	20°32	S 28
M29	14 29 46	9°10'15	7♑54	16°28	29°25	28°44	23°39	16°28	22°16	28°52	2° 6	15°24	14°35	23°12	20°35	M29
T 30	14 33 43	10♉ 8'32	21♑18	16♈47	0♉38	29♓30	23♉53	16♓33	22♉20	28♓54	2♒ 6	15♈22	14♈31	23♍18	20♈39	T 30

Delta T = 69.08 sec

MAY 2024 **00:00 UT**

Day	Sid.t	☉	☽	☿	♀	♂	♃	♄	♅	♆	♇	☊	Ω	⚸	⚷	Day
W 1	14 37 40	11♉ 6'48	4♒58	17♈11	1♉52	0♈16	24♉ 7	16♓38	22♉23	28♓56	2♒ 6	15°D21	14♈28	23♍25	20♈42	W 1
T 2	14 41 36	12° 5'02	18°53	17°39	3° 6	1° 3	24°21	16°43	22°27	28°58	2° 6	15♈21	14°25	23°32	20°45	T 2
F 3	14 45 33	13° 3'15	3♓ 3	18°11	4°20	1°49	24°35	16°49	22°30	28°59	2°R 6	15°22	14°22	23°38	20°49	F 3
S 4	14 49 29	14° 1'26	17°27	18°47	5°34	2°35	24°49	16°54	22°34	29° 1	2° 6	15°23	14°19	23°45	20°52	S 4
S 5	14 53 26	14°59'36	2♈ 2	19°26	6°48	3°21	25° 4	16°59	22°37	29° 3	2° 6	15°24	14°15	23°52	20°55	S 5
M 6	14 57 22	15°57'44	16°43	20°10	8° 2	4° 7	25°18	17° 4	22°41	29° 4	2° 6	15°R25	14°12	23°58	20°59	M 6
T 7	15 1 19	16°55'50	1♉24	20°57	9°16	4°53	25°32	17° 8	22°44	29° 6	2° 6	15°24	14° 9	24° 5	21° 2	T 7
W 8	15 5 15	17°53'56	16° 0	21°48	10°30	5°39	25°46	17°13	22°47	29° 8	2° 6	15°22	14° 6	24°12	21° 5	W 8
T 9	15 9 12	18°51'59	0♊23	22°42	11°44	6°25	26° 0	17°18	22°51	29° 9	2° 6	15°18	14° 3	24°18	21° 8	T 9
F 10	15 13 9	19°50'01	14°29	23°39	12°57	7°11	26°14	17°23	22°54	29°11	2° 5	15°13	14° 0	24°25	21°12	F 10
S 11	15 17 5	20°48'02	28°12	24°39	14°11	7°57	26°28	17°27	22°58	29°13	2° 5	15° 7	13°56	24°32	21°15	S 11
S 12	15 21 2	21°46'00	11♋30	25°42	15°25	8°43	26°42	17°32	23° 1	29°14	2° 5	15° 2	13°53	24°38	21°18	S 12
M13	15 24 58	22°43'57	24°25	26°48	16°39	9°29	26°57	17°36	23° 5	29°16	2° 5	14°57	13°50	24°45	21°21	M13
T 14	15 28 55	23°41'52	6♌58	27°56	17°53	10°15	27°11	17°41	23° 8	29°17	2° 4	14°54	13°47	24°51	21°24	T 14
W15	15 32 51	24°39'45	19°12	29° 8	19° 7	11° 1	27°25	17°45	23°12	29°19	2° 4	14°D53	13°44	24°58	21°27	W15
T 16	15 36 48	25°37'37	1♍13	0♉22	20°20	11°46	27°39	17°49	23°15	29°20	2° 4	14°53	13°41	25° 5	21°30	T 16
F 17	15 40 44	26°35'26	13° 5	1°38	21°34	12°32	27°53	17°53	23°19	29°22	2° 3	14°54	13°37	25°11	21°33	F 17
S 18	15 44 41	27°33'14	24°54	2°57	22°48	13°18	28° 7	17°57	23°22	29°23	2° 3	14°55	13°34	25°18	21°36	S 18
S 19	15 48 38	28°31'00	6♎43	4°19	24° 2	14° 3	28°21	18° 1	23°26	29°24	2° 3	14°56	13°31	25°25	21°39	S 19
M20	15 52 34	29°28'45	18°39	5°43	25°16	14°49	28°36	18° 5	23°29	29°26	2° 2	14°R57	13°28	25°31	21°42	M20
T 21	15 56 31	0♊26'28	0♏44	7° 9	26°29	15°35	28°50	18° 9	23°33	29°27	2° 2	14°55	13°25	25°38	21°45	T 21
W22	16 0 27	1°24'10	13° 1	8°38	27°43	16°20	29° 4	18°12	23°36	29°28	2° 1	14°52	13°21	25°45	21°48	W22
T 23	16 4 24	2°21'50	25°33	10° 9	28°57	17° 6	29°18	18°16	23°40	29°30	2° 1	14°47	13°18	25°51	21°51	T 23
F 24	16 8 20	3°19'29	8♐21	11°42	0♊11	17°51	29°32	18°20	23°43	29°31	2° 0	14°39	13°15	25°58	21°54	F 24
S 25	16 12 17	4°17'07	21°23	13°18	1°25	18°36	29°46	18°23	23°47	29°32	1°59	14°31	13°12	26° 5	21°57	S 25
S 26	16 16 13	5°14'44	4♑41	14°56	2°38	19°22	0♊ 0	18°26	23°50	29°33	1°59	14°23	13° 9	26°11	22° 0	S 26
M27	16 20 10	6°12'20	18°11	16°36	3°52	20° 7	0°15	18°30	23°53	29°35	1°58	14°15	13° 6	26°18	22° 2	M27
T 28	16 24 7	7° 9'55	1♒52	18°19	5° 6	20°52	0°29	18°33	23°57	29°36	1°58	14° 9	13° 2	26°25	22° 5	T 28
W29	16 28 3	8° 7'28	15°43	20° 4	6°20	21°37	0°43	18°36	24° 0	29°37	1°57	14° 4	12°59	26°31	22° 8	W29
T 30	16 32 0	9° 5'01	29°41	21°51	7°33	22°23	0°57	18°39	24° 4	29°38	1°56	14° 2	12°56	26°38	22°11	T 30
F 31	16 35 56	10♊ 2'33	13♓46	23♉41	8♊47	23♈ 8	1♊11	18♓42	24♉ 7	29♓39	1♒55	14°D 2	12♈53	26♍45	22♈13	F 31

Delta T = 69.07 sec

JUNE 2024 — 00:00 UT

Day	Sid.t	☉	☽	☿	♀	♂	♃	♄	♅	♆	♇	☊	☊	⚸	⚷	Day
S 1	16 39 53	11♊ 0'04	27♓57	25♉32	10♊ 1	23♈53	1♊25	18♓45	24♉10	29♓40	1°R55	14♈ 2	12♈50	26♍51	22♈16	S 1
S 2	16 43 49	11°57'35	12♈11	27°26	11°15	24°38	1°39	18°48	24°14	29°41	1♒54	14°R 3	12°47	26°58	22°18	S 2
M 3	16 47 46	12°55'04	26°28	29°23	12°28	25°23	1°53	18°50	24°17	29°42	1°53	14° 2	12°43	27° 5	22°21	M 3
T 4	16 51 42	13°52'33	10♉45	1♊21	13°42	26° 8	2° 7	18°53	24°20	29°43	1°52	14° 0	12°40	27°11	22°23	T 4
W 5	16 55 39	14°50'02	24°57	3°22	14°56	26°53	2°21	18°55	24°24	29°44	1°51	13°55	12°37	27°18	22°26	W 5
T 6	16 59 36	15°47'29	8♊59	5°24	16°10	27°37	2°35	18°58	24°27	29°45	1°51	13°47	12°34	27°24	22°28	T 6
F 7	17 3 32	16°44'56	22°49	7°28	17°23	28°22	2°49	19° 0	24°30	29°45	1°50	13°38	12°31	27°31	22°31	F 7
S 8	17 7 29	17°42'22	6♋20	9°34	18°37	29° 7	3° 3	19° 2	24°34	29°46	1°49	13°27	12°27	27°38	22°33	S 8
S 9	17 11 25	18°39'46	19°32	11°42	19°51	29°51	3°17	19° 4	24°37	29°47	1°48	13°17	12°24	27°44	22°35	S 9
M10	17 15 22	19°37'10	2♌24	13°51	21° 4	0♉36	3°30	19° 6	24°40	29°48	1°47	13° 7	12°21	27°51	22°37	M10
T11	17 19 18	20°34'33	14°55	16° 1	22°18	1°21	3°44	19° 8	24°43	29°48	1°46	13° 0	12°18	27°58	22°40	T11
W12	17 23 15	21°31'55	27° 9	18°12	23°32	2° 5	3°58	19°10	24°47	29°49	1°45	12°55	12°15	28° 4	22°42	W12
T13	17 27 11	22°29'16	9♍10	20°23	24°46	2°49	4°12	19°12	24°50	29°50	1°44	12°52	12°12	28°11	22°44	T13
F14	17 31 8	23°26'35	21° 2	22°35	25°59	3°34	4°25	19°13	24°53	29°50	1°43	12°D52	12° 8	28°18	22°46	F14
S15	17 35 5	24°23'54	2♎51	24°47	27°13	4°18	4°39	19°15	24°56	29°51	1°42	12°52	12° 5	28°24	22°48	S15
S16	17 39 1	25°21'12	14°42	26°59	28°27	5° 2	4°53	19°16	24°59	29°52	1°41	12°R52	12° 2	28°31	22°50	S16
M17	17 42 58	26°18'29	26°40	29°10	29°41	5°46	5° 6	19°18	25° 2	29°52	1°40	12°51	11°59	28°38	22°52	M17
T18	17 46 54	27°15'46	8♏50	1♋21	0♋54	6°30	5°20	19°19	25° 5	29°53	1°39	12°48	11°56	28°44	22°54	T18
W19	17 50 51	28°13'01	21°16	3°31	2° 8	7°14	5°34	19°20	25° 8	29°53	1°37	12°43	11°53	28°51	22°56	W19
T20	17 54 47	29°10'16	4♐ 0	5°39	3°22	7°58	5°47	19°21	25°12	29°53	1°36	12°36	11°49	28°58	22°58	T20
F21	17 58 44	0♋ 7'31	17° 5	7°46	4°35	8°42	6° 1	19°22	25°15	29°54	1°35	12°26	11°46	29° 4	23° 0	F21
S22	18 2 40	1° 4'45	0♑29	9°52	5°49	9°26	6°14	19°23	25°18	29°54	1°34	12°15	11°43	29°11	23° 1	S22
S23	18 6 37	2° 1'58	14°11	11°56	7° 3	10°10	6°27	19°23	25°20	29°54	1°33	12° 3	11°40	29°18	23° 3	S23
M24	18 10 34	2°59'12	28° 6	13°58	8°17	10°54	6°41	19°24	25°23	29°55	1°32	11°52	11°37	29°24	23° 5	M24
T25	18 14 30	3°56'25	12♒12	15°59	9°30	11°37	6°54	19°25	25°26	29°55	1°30	11°43	11°33	29°31	23° 6	T25
W26	18 18 27	4°53'37	26°22	17°57	10°44	12°21	7° 7	19°25	25°29	29°55	1°29	11°36	11°30	29°37	23° 8	W26
T27	18 22 23	5°50'50	10♓35	19°53	11°58	13° 4	7°21	19°25	25°32	29°55	1°28	11°32	11°27	29°44	23° 9	T27
F28	18 26 20	6°48'03	24°46	21°48	13°11	13°48	7°34	19°26	25°35	29°56	1°27	11°31	11°24	29°51	23°11	F28
S29	18 30 16	7°45'15	8♈55	23°40	14°25	14°31	7°47	19°26	25°38	29°56	1°25	11°31	11°21	29°57	23°12	S29
S30	18 34 13	8♋42'28	22♈59	25♋30	15♋39	15♉14	8♊ 0	19°R26	25♉40	29♓56	1♒24	11♈30	11♈18	0♎ 4	23♈14	S30

Delta T = 69.06 sec

JULY 2024 — 00:00 UT

Day	Sid.t	☉	☽	☿	♀	♂	♃	♄	♅	♆	♇	☊	☊	⚸	⚷	Day
M 1	18 38 10	9♋39'41	6♉59	27♋18	16♋53	15♉58	8♊13	19°R26	25♉43	29♓56	1°R23	11°R29	11♈14	0♎11	23♈15	M 1
T 2	18 42 6	10°36'55	20°53	29° 4	18° 6	16°41	8°26	19♓25	25°46	29°R56	1♒22	11♈26	11°11	0°17	23°16	T 2
W 3	18 46 3	11°34'08	4♊40	0♌48	19°20	17°24	8°39	19°25	25°49	29°56	1°20	11°19	11° 8	0°24	23°18	W 3
T 4	18 49 59	12°31'22	18°18	2°30	20°34	18° 7	8°52	19°25	25°51	29°56	1°19	11°10	11° 5	0°31	23°19	T 4
F 5	18 53 56	13°28'35	1♋45	4° 9	21°47	18°50	9° 5	19°24	25°54	29°56	1°18	10°59	11° 2	0°37	23°20	F 5
S 6	18 57 52	14°25'49	14°57	5°47	23° 1	19°33	9°17	19°24	25°56	29°56	1°16	10°46	10°59	0°44	23°21	S 6
S 7	19 1 49	15°23'03	27°54	7°22	24°15	20°16	9°30	19°23	25°59	29°56	1°15	10°34	10°55	0°51	23°22	S 7
M 8	19 5 45	16°20'17	10♌35	8°55	25°29	20°58	9°43	19°22	26° 2	29°55	1°14	10°22	10°52	0°57	23°23	M 8
T 9	19 9 42	17°17'30	22°59	10°26	26°42	21°41	9°55	19°21	26° 4	29°55	1°12	10°13	10°49	1° 4	23°24	T 9
W10	19 13 39	18°14'44	5♍ 9	11°55	27°56	22°23	10° 8	19°21	26° 6	29°55	1°11	10° 6	10°46	1°11	23°25	W10
T 11	19 17 35	19°11'57	17° 7	13°22	29°10	23° 6	10°20	19°19	26° 9	29°55	1° 9	10° 2	10°43	1°17	23°26	T 11
F 12	19 21 32	20° 9'11	28°58	14°46	0♌24	23°48	10°33	19°18	26°11	29°54	1° 8	10° 0	10°39	1°24	23°26	F 12
S 13	19 25 28	21° 6'24	10♎46	16° 8	1°37	24°30	10°45	19°17	26°14	29°54	1° 7	10°D 0	10°36	1°30	23°27	S 13
S 14	19 29 25	22° 3'38	22°36	17°28	2°51	25°13	10°57	19°16	26°16	29°54	1° 5	10°R 0	10°33	1°37	23°28	S 14
M15	19 33 21	23° 0'51	4♏34	18°45	4° 5	25°55	11° 9	19°14	26°18	29°53	1° 4	10° 0	10°30	1°44	23°29	M15
T 16	19 37 18	23°58'05	16°46	20° 0	5°19	26°37	11°21	19°13	26°20	29°53	1° 2	9°58	10°27	1°50	23°29	T 16
W17	19 41 14	24°55'19	29°15	21°13	6°32	27°19	11°33	19°11	26°23	29°52	1° 1	9°53	10°24	1°57	23°30	W17
T 18	19 45 11	25°52'33	12♐ 6	22°23	7°46	28° 1	11°45	19° 9	26°25	29°52	1° 0	9°47	10°20	2° 4	23°30	T 18
F 19	19 49 8	26°49'47	25°22	23°31	9° 0	28°42	11°57	19° 8	26°27	29°51	0°58	9°38	10°17	2°10	23°31	F 19
S 20	19 53 4	27°47'02	9♑ 1	24°36	10°13	29°24	12° 9	19° 6	26°29	29°51	0°57	9°28	10°14	2°17	23°31	S 20
S 21	19 57 1	28°44'17	23° 3	25°38	11°27	0♊ 6	12°21	19° 4	26°31	29°50	0°55	9°17	10°11	2°24	23°31	S 21
M22	20 0 57	29°41'32	7♒21	26°37	12°41	0°47	12°32	19° 2	26°33	29°50	0°54	9° 7	10° 8	2°30	23°32	M22
T 23	20 4 54	0♌38'48	21°52	27°33	13°55	1°29	12°44	18°59	26°35	29°49	0°53	8°58	10° 5	2°37	23°32	T 23
W24	20 8 50	1°36'04	6♓27	28°26	15° 8	2°10	12°55	18°57	26°37	29°48	0°51	8°52	10° 1	2°44	23°32	W24
T 25	20 12 47	2°33'22	21° 1	29°16	16°22	2°51	13° 7	18°55	26°39	29°48	0°50	8°49	9°58	2°50	23°32	T 25
F 26	20 16 43	3°30'40	5♈29	0♍ 2	17°36	3°32	13°18	18°52	26°40	29°47	0°48	8°D48	9°55	2°57	23°32	F 26
S 27	20 20 40	4°27'59	19°46	0°45	18°49	4°13	13°29	18°50	26°42	29°46	0°47	8°48	9°52	3° 4	23°R32	S 27
S 28	20 24 37	5°25'19	3♉52	1°25	20° 3	4°54	13°40	18°47	26°44	29°46	0°45	8°R48	9°49	3°10	23°32	S 28
M29	20 28 33	6°22'40	17°45	2° 0	21°17	5°35	13°51	18°44	26°46	29°45	0°44	8°48	9°45	3°17	23°32	M29
T 30	20 32 30	7°20'02	1♊26	2°32	22°30	6°16	14° 2	18°42	26°47	29°44	0°43	8°46	9°42	3°23	23°32	T 30
W31	20 36 26	8♌17'26	14♊55	2♍59	23♌44	6♊57	14♊13	18♓39	26♉49	29♓43	0♒41	8♈41	9♈39	3♎30	23♈32	W31

Delta T = 69.05 sec

AUGUST 2024 00:00 UT

Day	Sid.t	☉	☽	☿	♀	♂	♃	♄	♅	♆	♇	☊	☊	⚸	⚷	Day
T 1	20 40 23	9♌14'50	28♊11	3♍22	24♌58	7♊37	14♊24	18°R36	26♉51	29°R42	0°R40	8°R34	9♈36	3♎37	23°R31	T 1
F 2	20 44 19	10°12'16	11♋15	3°40	26°12	8°18	14°35	18♓33	26°52	29♓41	0♒38	8♈25	9°33	3°43	23♈31	F 2
S 3	20 48 16	11° 9'42	24° 6	3°54	27°25	8°58	14°45	18°30	26°54	29°40	0°37	8°15	9°30	3°50	23°31	S 3
S 4	20 52 13	12° 7'10	6♌44	4° 3	28°39	9°39	14°56	18°27	26°55	29°39	0°36	8° 5	9°26	3°57	23°30	S 4
M 5	20 56 9	13° 4'38	19° 9	4°R 6	29°53	10°19	15° 6	18°23	26°56	29°38	0°34	7°56	9°23	4° 3	23°30	M 5
T 6	21 0 6	14° 2'08	1♍23	4° 5	1♍ 6	10°59	15°16	18°20	26°58	29°37	0°33	7°48	9°20	4°10	23°29	T 6
W 7	21 4 2	14°59'38	13°25	3°58	2°20	11°39	15°27	18°17	26°59	29°36	0°32	7°43	9°17	4°17	23°29	W 7
T 8	21 7 59	15°57'09	25°19	3°46	3°34	12°19	15°37	18°13	27° 0	29°35	0°30	7°40	9°14	4°23	23°28	T 8
F 9	21 11 55	16°54'41	7♎ 7	3°28	4°47	12°58	15°47	18°10	27° 1	29°34	0°29	7°D39	9°11	4°30	23°27	F 9
S 10	21 15 52	17°52'13	18°53	3° 5	6° 1	13°38	15°56	18° 6	27° 3	29°33	0°27	7°40	9° 7	4°37	23°27	S 10
S 11	21 19 48	18°49'47	0♏43	2°37	7°15	14°18	16° 6	18° 2	27° 4	29°32	0°26	7°41	9° 4	4°43	23°26	S 11
M12	21 23 45	19°47'22	12°40	2° 5	8°28	14°57	16°16	17°59	27° 5	29°31	0°25	7°42	9° 1	4°50	23°25	M12
T 13	21 27 41	20°44'57	24°50	1°27	9°42	15°36	16°25	17°55	27° 6	29°30	0°23	7°R42	8°58	4°57	23°24	T 13
W14	21 31 38	21°42'34	7♐19	0°46	10°56	16°15	16°35	17°51	27° 7	29°28	0°22	7°41	8°55	5° 3	23°23	W14
T 15	21 35 35	22°40'11	20°10	0° 1	12° 9	16°55	16°44	17°47	27° 8	29°27	0°21	7°38	8°51	5°10	23°22	T 15
F 16	21 39 31	23°37'50	3♑27	29♌13	13°23	17°33	16°53	17°43	27° 8	29°26	0°20	7°33	8°48	5°16	23°21	F 16
S 17	21 43 28	24°35'30	17°11	28°23	14°37	18°12	17° 2	17°39	27° 9	29°25	0°18	7°27	8°45	5°23	23°20	S 17
S 18	21 47 24	25°33'10	1♒21	27°31	15°50	18°51	17°11	17°35	27°10	29°23	0°17	7°20	8°42	5°30	23°19	S 18
M19	21 51 21	26°30'52	15°54	26°40	17° 4	19°30	17°20	17°31	27°11	29°22	0°16	7°14	8°39	5°36	23°18	M19
T 20	21 55 17	27°28'35	0♓43	25°49	18°17	20° 8	17°28	17°27	27°11	29°21	0°15	7° 9	8°36	5°43	23°17	T 20
W21	21 59 14	28°26'19	15°40	25° 0	19°31	20°47	17°37	17°23	27°12	29°19	0°13	7° 6	8°32	5°50	23°15	W21
T 22	22 3 10	29°24'05	0♈36	24°14	20°44	21°25	17°45	17°19	27°13	29°18	0°12	7°D 4	8°29	5°56	23°14	T 22
F 23	22 7 7	0♍21'52	15°25	23°32	21°58	22° 3	17°53	17°14	27°13	29°16	0°11	7° 4	8°26	6° 3	23°13	F 23
S 24	22 11 4	1°19'41	29°59	22°54	23°11	22°41	18° 2	17°10	27°13	29°15	0°10	7° 5	8°23	6°10	23°11	S 24
S 25	22 15 0	2°17'32	14♉17	22°23	24°25	23°19	18° 9	17° 6	27°14	29°14	0° 9	7° 7	8°20	6°16	23°10	S 25
M26	22 18 57	3°15'25	28°14	21°57	25°39	23°56	18°17	17° 1	27°14	29°12	0° 8	7°R 8	8°16	6°23	23° 8	M26
T 27	22 22 53	4°13'20	11♊52	21°39	26°52	24°34	18°25	16°57	27°15	29°11	0° 6	7° 8	8°13	6°30	23° 7	T 27
W28	22 26 50	5°11'16	25°12	21°28	28° 6	25°12	18°33	16°53	27°15	29° 9	0° 5	7° 6	8°10	6°36	23° 5	W28
T 29	22 30 46	6° 9'14	8♋14	21°D25	29°19	25°49	18°40	16°48	27°15	29° 8	0° 4	7° 3	8° 7	6°43	23° 4	T 29
F 30	22 34 43	7° 7'14	21° 0	21°30	0♎33	26°26	18°47	16°44	27°15	29° 6	0° 3	6°59	8° 4	6°49	23° 2	F 30
S 31	22 38 40	8♍ 5'16	3♌33	21♌43	1♎46	27♊ 3	18♊54	16♓39	27♉15	29♓ 5	0♒ 2	6♈54	8♈ 1	6♎56	23♈ 0	S 31

Delta T = 69.04 sec

SEPTEMBER 2024

00:00 UT

Day	Sid.t	☉	☽	☿	♀	♂	♃	♄	♅	♆	♇	☊	Ω	⚸	⚷	Day
S 1	22 42 36	9♍ 3'20	15♌54	22♌ 5	2♎59	27♊40	19♊ 1	16°R35	27♉15	29°R 3	0°R 1	6°R50	7♈57	7♎ 3	22°R58	S 1
M 2	22 46 33	10° 1'25	28° 5	22°35	4°13	28°17	19° 8	16♓30	27°R15	29♓ 2	29♑59	6♈45	7°54	7° 9	22♈57	M 2
T 3	22 50 29	10°59'32	10♍ 7	23°13	5°26	28°54	19°15	16°25	27°15	29° 0	29°59	6°42	7°51	7°16	22°55	T 3
W 4	22 54 26	11°57'40	22° 1	23°59	6°40	29°30	19°21	16°21	27°15	28°59	29°58	6°40	7°48	7°23	22°53	W 4
T 5	22 58 22	12°55'50	3♎50	24°53	7°53	0♋ 6	19°28	16°16	27°15	28°57	29°57	6°D39	7°45	7°29	22°51	T 5
F 6	23 2 19	13°54'02	15°37	25°54	9° 7	0°43	19°34	16°12	27°15	28°55	29°56	6°39	7°42	7°36	22°49	F 6
S 7	23 6 15	14°52'16	27°23	27° 2	10°20	1°19	19°40	16° 7	27°15	28°54	29°55	6°40	7°38	7°43	22°47	S 7
S 8	23 10 12	15°50'31	9♏14	28°16	11°33	1°54	19°46	16° 3	27°14	28°52	29°54	6°42	7°35	7°49	22°45	S 8
M 9	23 14 8	16°48'47	21°12	29°36	12°47	2°30	19°52	15°58	27°14	28°51	29°53	6°43	7°32	7°56	22°43	M 9
T 10	23 18 5	17°47'06	3♐21	1♍ 2	14° 0	3° 6	19°57	15°53	27°14	28°49	29°53	6°45	7°29	8° 3	22°41	T 10
W11	23 22 2	18°45'25	15°48	2°32	15°13	3°41	20° 3	15°49	27°13	28°47	29°52	6°R45	7°26	8° 9	22°39	W11
T 12	23 25 58	19°43'47	28°35	4° 7	16°27	4°16	20° 8	15°44	27°13	28°46	29°51	6°45	7°22	8°16	22°37	T 12
F 13	23 29 55	20°42'10	11♑46	5°45	17°40	4°51	20°13	15°40	27°12	28°44	29°50	6°44	7°19	8°22	22°34	F 13
S 14	23 33 51	21°40'34	25°25	7°27	18°53	5°26	20°18	15°35	27°12	28°43	29°49	6°43	7°16	8°29	22°32	S 14
S 15	23 37 48	22°39'00	9♒31	9°11	20° 7	6° 1	20°23	15°30	27°11	28°41	29°49	6°41	7°13	8°36	22°30	S 15
M16	23 41 44	23°37'28	24° 3	10°57	21°20	6°35	20°27	15°26	27°10	28°39	29°48	6°39	7°10	8°42	22°28	M16
T 17	23 45 41	24°35'57	8♓56	12°45	22°33	7°10	20°32	15°21	27° 9	28°38	29°47	6°38	7° 7	8°49	22°25	T 17
W18	23 49 37	25°34'28	24° 3	14°35	23°46	7°44	20°36	15°17	27° 9	28°36	29°47	6°37	7° 3	8°56	22°23	W18
T 19	23 53 34	26°33'01	9♈15	16°25	25° 0	8°18	20°40	15°12	27° 8	28°34	29°46	6°D37	7° 0	9° 2	22°20	T 19
F 20	23 57 31	27°31'36	24°21	18°16	26°13	8°52	20°44	15° 8	27° 7	28°33	29°45	6°37	6°57	9° 9	22°18	F 20
S 21	0 1 27	28°30'13	9♉15	20° 7	27°26	9°26	20°47	15° 4	27° 6	28°31	29°45	6°38	6°54	9°16	22°16	S 21
S 22	0 5 24	29°28'53	23°49	21°59	28°39	9°59	20°51	14°59	27° 5	28°29	29°44	6°38	6°51	9°22	22°13	S 22
M23	0 9 20	0♎27'34	7♊58	23°50	29°52	10°32	20°54	14°55	27° 4	28°28	29°44	6°39	6°48	9°29	22°11	M23
T 24	0 13 17	1°26'18	21°43	25°42	1♏ 5	11° 5	20°57	14°51	27° 3	28°26	29°43	6°39	6°44	9°36	22° 8	T 24
W25	0 17 13	2°25'04	5♋ 3	27°32	2°18	11°38	21° 0	14°46	27° 2	28°24	29°43	6°R39	6°41	9°42	22° 6	W25
T 26	0 21 10	3°23'53	18° 0	29°23	3°31	12°11	21° 3	14°42	27° 1	28°23	29°42	6°39	6°38	9°49	22° 3	T 26
F 27	0 25 6	4°22'44	0♌38	1♎12	4°44	12°43	21° 5	14°38	27° 0	28°21	29°42	6°39	6°35	9°56	22° 0	F 27
S 28	0 29 3	5°21'37	13° 0	3° 1	5°57	13°16	21° 8	14°34	26°58	28°19	29°41	6°39	6°32	10° 2	21°58	S 28
S 29	0 33 0	6°20'32	25° 8	4°50	7°10	13°48	21°10	14°30	26°57	28°18	29°41	6°D39	6°28	10° 9	21°55	S 29
M30	0 36 56	7♎19'29	7♍ 8	6♎37	8♏23	14♋19	21♊12	14♓26	26♉56	28♓16	29♑41	6♈39	6♈25	10♎15	21♈53	M30

Delta T = 69.03 sec

Day	Sid.t	☉	☽	☿	♀	♂	♃	♄	♅	♆	♇	☊	☊	⚸	⚷	Day
T 1	0 40 53	8♎18'28	19♍ 1	8♎24	9♏36	14♋51	21♊13	14°R22	26°R54	28°R14	29°R40	6♈39	6♈22	10♎22	21°R50	T 1
W 2	0 44 49	9°17'30	0♎49	10°10	10°49	15°22	21°15	14♓18	26♉53	28♓13	29♑40	6°R39	6°19	10°29	21♈47	W 2
T 3	0 48 46	10°16'33	12°36	11°55	12° 2	15°53	21°16	14°14	26°51	28°11	29°40	6°39	6°16	10°35	21°45	T 3
F 4	0 52 42	11°15'39	24°24	13°39	13°15	16°24	21°17	14°10	26°50	28°10	29°39	6°39	6°13	10°42	21°42	F 4
S 5	0 56 39	12°14'46	6♏14	15°23	14°28	16°55	21°18	14° 6	26°48	28° 8	29°39	6°38	6° 9	10°49	21°39	S 5
S 6	1 0 35	13°13'56	18°10	17° 6	15°41	17°25	21°19	14° 2	26°47	28° 6	29°39	6°37	6° 6	10°55	21°37	S 6
M 7	1 4 32	14°13'07	0♐13	18°47	16°54	17°56	21°20	13°59	26°45	28° 5	29°39	6°36	6° 3	11° 2	21°34	M 7
T 8	1 8 29	15°12'21	12°27	20°28	18° 7	18°25	21°20	13°55	26°43	28° 3	29°39	6°35	6° 0	11° 9	21°31	T 8
W 9	1 12 25	16°11'36	24°55	22° 9	19°20	18°55	21°R20	13°52	26°42	28° 2	29°39	6°34	5°57	11°15	21°28	W 9
T 10	1 16 22	17°10'53	7♑40	23°48	20°32	19°24	21°20	13°48	26°40	28° 0	29°39	6°34	5°54	11°22	21°26	T 10
F 11	1 20 18	18°10'12	20°46	25°27	21°45	19°53	21°20	13°45	26°38	27°59	29°39	6°D34	5°50	11°29	21°23	F 11
S 12	1 24 15	19° 9'32	4♒15	27° 5	22°58	20°22	21°20	13°41	26°36	27°57	29°D39	6°34	5°47	11°35	21°20	S 12
S 13	1 28 11	20° 8'54	18° 9	28°42	24°11	20°51	21°19	13°38	26°35	27°56	29°39	6°35	5°44	11°42	21°17	S 13
M14	1 32 8	21° 8'18	2♓28	0♏18	25°23	21°19	21°18	13°35	26°33	27°54	29°39	6°36	5°41	11°48	21°15	M14
T 15	1 36 4	22° 7'44	17°10	1°54	26°36	21°47	21°17	13°32	26°31	27°53	29°39	6°37	5°38	11°55	21°12	T 15
W16	1 40 1	23° 7'11	2♈ 9	3°29	27°49	22°15	21°16	13°29	26°29	27°51	29°39	6°R38	5°34	12° 2	21° 9	W16
T 17	1 43 58	24° 6'41	17°20	5° 4	29° 1	22°42	21°14	13°26	26°27	27°50	29°39	6°37	5°31	12° 8	21° 6	T 17
F 18	1 47 54	25° 6'12	2♉32	6°38	0♐14	23° 9	21°13	13°23	26°25	27°48	29°39	6°36	5°28	12°15	21° 4	F 18
S 19	1 51 51	26° 5'46	17°35	8°11	1°26	23°36	21°11	13°20	26°23	27°47	29°39	6°34	5°25	12°22	21° 1	S 19
S 20	1 55 47	27° 5'21	2♊22	9°44	2°39	24° 2	21° 9	13°18	26°21	27°45	29°39	6°32	5°22	12°28	20°58	S 20
M21	1 59 44	28° 4'59	16°45	11°16	3°51	24°29	21° 7	13°15	26°19	27°44	29°40	6°29	5°19	12°35	20°56	M21
T 22	2 3 40	29° 4'39	0♋40	12°47	5° 4	24°54	21° 4	13°13	26°17	27°43	29°40	6°26	5°15	12°42	20°53	T 22
W23	2 7 37	0♏ 4'22	14° 7	14°18	6°16	25°20	21° 1	13°10	26°14	27°41	29°40	6°24	5°12	12°48	20°50	W23
T 24	2 11 33	1° 4'07	27° 8	15°48	7°28	25°45	20°59	13° 8	26°12	27°40	29°41	6°D23	5° 9	12°55	20°47	T 24
F 25	2 15 30	2° 3'54	9♌45	17°18	8°41	26°10	20°56	13° 6	26°10	27°39	29°41	6°23	5° 6	13° 2	20°45	F 25
S 26	2 19 27	3° 3'43	22° 3	18°47	9°53	26°34	20°52	13° 4	26° 8	27°37	29°41	6°24	5° 3	13° 8	20°42	S 26
S 27	2 23 23	4° 3'34	4♍ 6	20°15	11° 5	26°58	20°49	13° 1	26° 6	27°36	29°42	6°26	4°59	13°15	20°39	S 27
M28	2 27 20	5° 3'27	16° 0	21°43	12°18	27°22	20°45	13° 0	26° 3	27°35	29°42	6°28	4°56	13°22	20°37	M28
T 29	2 31 16	6° 3'23	27°48	23°10	13°30	27°45	20°42	12°58	26° 1	27°34	29°43	6°29	4°53	13°28	20°34	T 29
W30	2 35 13	7° 3'21	9♎34	24°37	14°42	28° 8	20°38	12°56	25°59	27°32	29°43	6°R30	4°50	13°35	20°31	W30
T 31	2 39 9	8♏ 3'20	21♎22	26♏ 3	15♐54	28♋31	20♊33	12♓54	25♉56	27♓31	29♑44	6♈28	4♈47	13♎41	20♈29	T 31

Delta T = 69.03 sec

NOVEMBER 2024 00:00 UT

Day	Sid.t	☉	☽	☿	♀	♂	♃	♄	♅	♆	♇	☊	☊	⚸	⚷	Day
F 1	2 43 6	9♏ 3'22	3♏14	27♏28	17♐ 6	28♋53	20°R29	12°R53	25°R54	27°R30	29♑44	6°R26	4♈44	13♎48	20°R26	F 1
S 2	2 47 2	10° 3'26	15°12	28°53	18°18	29°14	20♊24	12♓51	25♉52	27♓29	29°45	6♈21	4°40	13°55	20♈24	S 2
S 3	2 50 59	11° 3'31	27°18	0♐16	19°30	29°36	20°20	12°50	25°49	27°28	29°45	6°15	4°37	14° 1	20°21	S 3
M 4	2 54 55	12° 3'39	9♐33	1°39	20°42	29°56	20°15	12°49	25°47	27°27	29°46	6° 9	4°34	14° 8	20°19	M 4
T 5	2 58 52	13° 3'48	21°59	3° 1	21°54	0♌17	20°10	12°47	25°44	27°26	29°47	6° 2	4°31	14°15	20°16	T 5
W 6	3 2 49	14° 3'58	4♑37	4°22	23° 6	0°37	20° 5	12°46	25°42	27°25	29°47	5°56	4°28	14°21	20°14	W 6
T 7	3 6 45	15° 4'11	17°28	5°42	24°18	0°56	19°59	12°45	25°40	27°24	29°48	5°51	4°25	14°28	20°11	T 7
F 8	3 10 42	16° 4'25	0♒34	7° 1	25°30	1°15	19°54	12°45	25°37	27°23	29°49	5°48	4°21	14°35	20° 9	F 8
S 9	3 14 38	17° 4'40	13°58	8°19	26°42	1°34	19°48	12°44	25°35	27°22	29°50	5°D47	4°18	14°41	20° 7	S 9
S 10	3 18 35	18° 4'57	27°41	9°35	27°53	1°51	19°42	12°43	25°32	27°21	29°51	5°47	4°15	14°48	20° 4	S 10
M11	3 22 31	19° 5'15	11♓44	10°50	29° 5	2° 9	19°36	12°43	25°30	27°20	29°51	5°48	4°12	14°55	20° 2	M11
T 12	3 26 28	20° 5'34	26° 6	12° 2	0♑17	2°26	19°30	12°42	25°27	27°19	29°52	5°50	4° 9	15° 1	20° 0	T 12
W13	3 30 25	21° 5'55	10♈46	13°13	1°28	2°42	19°24	12°42	25°25	27°18	29°53	5°R50	4° 5	15° 8	19°57	W13
T 14	3 34 21	22° 6'17	25°39	14°22	2°40	2°58	19°17	12°42	25°22	27°18	29°54	5°48	4° 2	15°14	19°55	T 14
F 15	3 38 18	23° 6'41	10♉38	15°28	3°51	3°14	19°11	12°42	25°20	27°17	29°55	5°44	3°59	15°21	19°53	F 15
S 16	3 42 14	24° 7'06	25°35	16°31	5° 2	3°28	19° 4	12°D42	25°17	27°16	29°56	5°39	3°56	15°28	19°51	S 16
S 17	3 46 11	25° 7'34	10♊21	17°31	6°14	3°43	18°57	12°42	25°15	27°15	29°57	5°31	3°53	15°34	19°49	S 17
M18	3 50 7	26° 8'02	24°47	18°28	7°25	3°56	18°50	12°42	25°12	27°15	29°58	5°22	3°50	15°41	19°46	M18
T 19	3 54 4	27° 8'33	8♋49	19°20	8°36	4°10	18°43	12°42	25°10	27°14	29°59	5°14	3°46	15°48	19°44	T 19
W20	3 58 0	28° 9'05	22°23	20° 8	9°47	4°22	18°36	12°43	25° 7	27°13	0♒ 0	5° 7	3°43	15°54	19°42	W20
T 21	4 1 57	29° 9'39	5♌29	20°50	10°58	4°34	18°29	12°43	25° 5	27°13	0° 1	5° 2	3°40	16° 1	19°40	T 21
F 22	4 5 54	0♐10'15	18°10	21°27	12° 9	4°45	18°21	12°44	25° 2	27°12	0° 2	5° 0	3°37	16° 8	19°38	F 22
S 23	4 9 50	1°10'52	0♍30	21°57	13°20	4°56	18°14	12°44	25° 0	27°12	0° 4	4°D59	3°34	16°14	19°37	S 23
S 24	4 13 47	2°11'31	12°33	22°20	14°30	5° 6	18° 6	12°45	24°57	27°11	0° 5	4°59	3°31	16°21	19°35	S 24
M25	4 17 43	3°12'12	24°26	22°34	15°41	5°15	17°59	12°46	24°55	27°11	0° 6	5° 0	3°27	16°28	19°33	M25
T 26	4 21 40	4°12'54	6♎13	22°R40	16°52	5°24	17°51	12°47	24°52	27°10	0° 7	5°R 0	3°24	16°34	19°31	T 26
W27	4 25 36	5°13'38	17°59	22°36	18° 2	5°32	17°43	12°48	24°50	27°10	0° 8	4°59	3°21	16°41	19°29	W27
T 28	4 29 33	6°14'23	29°50	22°22	19°13	5°39	17°35	12°50	24°47	27°10	0°10	4°56	3°18	16°48	19°28	T 28
F 29	4 33 29	7°15'10	11♏48	21°57	20°23	5°45	17°27	12°51	24°45	27° 9	0°11	4°50	3°15	16°54	19°26	F 29
S 30	4 37 26	8♐15'58	23♏55	21♐21	21♑33	5♌51	17♊19	12♓53	24♉43	27♓ 9	0♒12	4♈42	3♈11	17♎ 1	19♈24	S 30

Delta T = 69.02 sec

DECEMBER 2024 — 00:00 UT

Day	Sid.t	☉	☽	☿	♀	♂	♃	♄	♅	♆	♇	☊	☊	⚸	⚷	Day
S 1	4 41 23	9♐16'48	6♐15	20°R35	22♑43	5♌56	17°R11	12♓54	24°R40	27°R 9	0♒14	4°R31	3♈ 8	17♎ 8	19°R23	S 1
M 2	4 45 19	10°17'39	18°47	19♐37	23°53	6° 0	17♊ 3	12°56	24♉38	27♓ 8	0°15	4♈18	3° 5	17°14	19♈21	M 2
T 3	4 49 16	11°18'30	1♑31	18°31	25° 3	6° 4	16°55	12°58	24°35	27° 8	0°16	4° 6	3° 2	17°21	19°20	T 3
W 4	4 53 12	12°19'23	14°28	17°17	26°13	6° 7	16°47	12°59	24°33	27° 8	0°18	3°54	2°59	17°27	19°18	W 4
T 5	4 57 9	13°20'17	27°36	15°57	27°23	6° 9	16°39	13° 1	24°31	27° 8	0°19	3°44	2°56	17°34	19°17	T 5
F 6	5 1 5	14°21'12	10♒55	14°35	28°33	6°10	16°31	13° 4	24°28	27° 8	0°21	3°37	2°52	17°41	19°16	F 6
S 7	5 5 2	15°22'08	24°25	13°12	29°42	6°R10	16°23	13° 6	24°26	27° 8	0°22	3°33	2°49	17°47	19°15	S 7
S 8	5 8 58	16°23'04	8♓ 7	11°52	0♒51	6°10	16°14	13° 8	24°24	27°D 8	0°23	3°31	2°46	17°54	19°13	S 8
M 9	5 12 55	17°24'00	22° 1	10°37	2° 1	6° 9	16° 6	13°10	24°22	27° 8	0°25	3°D31	2°43	18° 1	19°12	M 9
T 10	5 16 52	18°24'58	6♈ 7	9°30	3°10	6° 7	15°58	13°13	24°19	27° 8	0°26	3°R31	2°40	18° 7	19°11	T 10
W11	5 20 48	19°25'56	20°25	8°32	4°19	6° 4	15°50	13°15	24°17	27° 8	0°28	3°30	2°37	18°14	19°10	W11
T 12	5 24 45	20°26'54	4♉53	7°44	5°27	6° 0	15°42	13°18	24°15	27° 8	0°30	3°27	2°33	18°21	19° 9	T 12
F 13	5 28 41	21°27'54	19°27	7° 8	6°36	5°56	15°34	13°21	24°13	27° 8	0°31	3°21	2°30	18°27	19° 8	F 13
S 14	5 32 38	22°28'53	4♊ 1	6°42	7°44	5°50	15°26	13°24	24°11	27° 8	0°33	3°12	2°27	18°34	19° 7	S 14
S 15	5 36 34	23°29'54	18°29	6°28	8°53	5°44	15°18	13°27	24° 9	27° 9	0°34	3° 1	2°24	18°41	19° 6	S 15
M16	5 40 31	24°30'55	2♋44	6°D24	10° 1	5°37	15°10	13°30	24° 7	27° 9	0°36	2°49	2°21	18°47	19° 5	M16
T 17	5 44 28	25°31'58	16°39	6°30	11° 9	5°29	15° 2	13°33	24° 5	27° 9	0°38	2°36	2°17	18°54	19° 5	T 17
W18	5 48 24	26°33'00	0♌12	6°45	12°16	5°20	14°54	13°36	24° 3	27°10	0°39	2°25	2°14	19° 1	19° 4	W18
T 19	5 52 21	27°34'04	13°19	7° 9	13°24	5°11	14°46	13°40	24° 1	27°10	0°41	2°16	2°11	19° 7	19° 3	T 19
F 20	5 56 17	28°35'08	26° 2	7°40	14°31	5° 1	14°38	13°43	23°59	27°10	0°43	2°10	2° 8	19°14	19° 3	F 20
S 21	6 0 14	29°36'13	8♍25	8°18	15°39	4°49	14°31	13°47	23°57	27°11	0°44	2° 7	2° 5	19°21	19° 2	S 21
S 22	6 4 10	0♑37'19	20°30	9° 2	16°46	4°37	14°23	13°50	23°55	27°11	0°46	2° 6	2° 2	19°27	19° 2	S 22
M23	6 8 7	1°38'25	2♎24	9°51	17°52	4°25	14°15	13°54	23°53	27°12	0°48	2° 6	1°58	19°34	19° 1	M23
T 24	6 12 3	2°39'32	14°12	10°45	18°59	4°11	14° 8	13°58	23°51	27°12	0°50	2° 5	1°55	19°41	19° 1	T 24
W25	6 16 0	3°40'40	26° 0	11°43	20° 5	3°57	14° 1	14° 2	23°49	27°13	0°51	2° 4	1°52	19°47	19° 1	W25
T 26	6 19 57	4°41'49	7♏53	12°45	21°11	3°41	13°54	14° 6	23°48	27°14	0°53	2° 0	1°49	19°54	19° 0	T 26
F 27	6 23 53	5°42'58	19°55	13°50	22°17	3°25	13°47	14°10	23°46	27°14	0°55	1°54	1°46	20° 0	19° 0	F 27
S 28	6 27 50	6°44'07	2♐11	14°58	23°23	3° 9	13°40	14°14	23°44	27°15	0°57	1°45	1°43	20° 7	19° 0	S 28
S 29	6 31 46	7°45'17	14°42	16° 9	24°28	2°51	13°33	14°18	23°43	27°16	0°58	1°33	1°39	20°14	19° 0	S 29
M30	6 35 43	8°46'28	27°30	17°21	25°33	2°33	13°26	14°23	23°41	27°16	1° 0	1°19	1°36	20°20	19°D 0	M30
T 31	6 39 39	9♑47'38	10♑35	18♐36	26♒38	2♌14	13♊19	14♓27	23♉40	27♓17	1♒ 2	1♈ 6	1♈33	20♎27	19♈ 0	T 31

Delta T = 69.01 sec

Quick Reference

2024 RETROGRADE MOTION OF PLANETS

MERCURY...Dec 12, 2023 11:08pm 8°♑ .... Jan 1, 7:07pm 22°♐
April 1, 3:14pm 27°♈............................ April 25th, 5:53am 15°♈
Aug 4, 9:55pm 4°♍.................................. Aug 28th, 2:13pm 21°♌
Nov 25, 6:42pm 22°♐............................. Dec 15, 12:56pm 6°♐
VENUS........................No Retrogrades for Venus in 2024..............................!
MARS..........Dec 6, 3:32pm 6°♌...........................Feb 23, 2025, 5:59pm 17°♋
JUPITER......Oct 9, 12:04am 21°♊....................... Feb 4, 2025, 1:40am 11°♊
SATURN.......Jun 29, 12:05pm 19°♓ .... Nov 15, 6:20am 12°♓
URANUS......Aug 28, 2023 7:38pm 23°♉....................Jan 26, 11:34pm 19°♉
URANUS......Sep 1, 8:17am 27°♉..........................Jan 30, 2025, 8:32am 23°♉
NEPTUNE....July 2, 3:40am 29°♓.................................. Dec 7, 3:42pm 27°♓
PLUTO.........May 2, 10:46am 2°♒ .... Oct 11, 5:31pm 29°♑

2024 ECLIPSES

Mar 25, 12:00am - Appulse Lunar 5° ♎| April 8, 11:20am - Total Solar 19°♈
Sep 17, 7:34pm - Partical Lunar 25° ♓ | Oct 2, 11:49am - Annular Solar 10° ♎

Timing: Start projects between the New and Full Moon because energy is rising. The Sun Trine Moon after the Full Moon (Waning Gibbous) is when the energy is flowing most smoothly so that's a good time to overcome resistance. As Planets prepare to change Direction they slow from our perspective and issues related to them in our world will be harder to move forward.

When the Planets are moving fast, you have the wind at your back. Everything related to them happens more quickly and easily. That is why it is important to understand what each Planet signifies. In our Forecasts, we also take into account the speed of the Planets as indicators. Some Planets change Sign and Direction more often.

Quick Reference: Timing

When Planets are above the Dotted Line actions are supported. Delay these actions when the Planets are below the Dotted Line.

☉ **SUN:** Time to ask favors from superiors, to have dealings with attorneys or government. Start publicity.

☽ **MOON:** Time to handle the public, straighten affairs at home and deal with women. Watch the four quarters of the moon for planting.

☿ **MERCURY:** Start writing, start publishing, start intellectual pursuits, study, learn. Deliver public addresses.

♀ **VENUS:** Commence romance, start to gain favor of the opposite sex. Buy jewelry, clothes. Participate in art, music or entertainment.

♂ **MARS:** Start work on machinery, undergo surgery, start construction, organize sales force. Advance business.

♃ **JUPITER:** Take care of money matters, sign contracts. Start or search for new business. Time to start speculating.

♄ **SATURN:** Start building projects, handle real estate deals, develop mining. Start repairing, plumbing and digging.

♅ **URANUS:** Begin experiments, inventions and new ideas. Start traveling, especially by air. Investigate important propositions.

♆ **NEPTUNE:** Start water trips, start brewing, mix strange chemicals. Start poetry, shipping, investigate secrets.

♇ **PLUTO:** Start organizations, foundations and new principles. Time to "turn over a new leaf."

Quick Reference: Signs & Planetary Rulers

BIRTH DATE SIGN ELEMENT QUALITY RULING PLANET

March 21 to April 19 ..... Aries ♈..... Fire ..... Cardinal .... Mars ♂

April 20 to May 20 .... Taurus ♉.. Earth .... Fixed .... Venus ♀

May 21 to June 20 .... Gemini ♊.... Air .... Mutable .... Mercury ☿

June 21 to July 22 .... Cancer ♋ .... Water .... Cardinal ... Moon ☽

July 23 to August 22 ...... Leo ♌ ..... Fire .... Fixed .... Sun ☉

August 23 to Sept 22 ... Virgo ♍ ... Earth ... Mutable..... Mercury ☿

Sept 23 to Oct 22 ..... Libra ♎ .... Air ..... Cardinal .... Venus ♀

Oct 23 to Nov 21 ...... Scorpio ♏..... Water ..... Fixed.....Tr. Mars ♂

Modern Ruler - Pluto ♇

Nov 22 to Dec 21 ... Sagittarius ♐.... Fire .... Mutable ..... Jupiter ♃

Dec 22 to Jan 19 .... Capricorn ♑.... Earth .... Cardinal .... Saturn ♄

Jan 20 to Feb 18 ..... Aquarius ♒ ..... Air ..... Fixed ..... Tr. Saturn ♄

Modern Ruler - Uranus ♅

Feb 19 to March 20 .. Pisces ♓.... Water... Mutable... Tr. Jupiter ♃

Modern Ruler - Neptune ♆

Traditional Ruling Signs from the Table of Dignities (pg. 15) are Signs where the Planet is most socially expressive in a Dynamic or Responsive manner. Note the Exaltation for the Sun is Aries and for the Moon is Taurus. Refer to page 8 for their daily application for Leos and Cancerians in place of the Sun and Moon.

Calendar Times are based on the Clock for Pacific Time, adjusting with Daylight Savings Time.

Made in the USA
Las Vegas, NV
07 January 2024

84017726R00049